Casanova Undone

Looking for the World

Long to Rain Over Us

Casanova Undone

Looking for the World

Long to Rain Over Us

Three plays by

Dic Edwards

Oberon Books

London • England

First published in 1992 by Oberon Books Limited
521 Caledonian Road, London N7.

Typeset in England by O'Reilly Clark Printing Services, Enfield
Printed by Latimer Trend & Co. Ltd., Plymouth
Text typeset in Garamond ITC
Front cover illustration by Peter Farmer

ISBN 1 870 259 29 7

Oberon Books Limited

521 Caledonian Road, London N7 England

Publishing Director: James Hogan
Managing Director: Charles Glanville
Associate Editor: Nicholas Dromgoole MA (Oxon), FIChor

822.914
Edw

Contents

Acknowledgments

Thank you so much Gwenda and Natalie. Thanks too to Amanda and Nicholas, Elizabeth Comstock-Smith – my agent, Andy Jordan and Bristol Express, Billy Adams and Made in Wales Stage Company, and Jack Elliott.

Introduction

Human beings seem to have little choice in their lives. We can't choose the parents, class, age, nation or culture we're born to. And we know surprisingly little of ourselves. We know that past societies destroyed themselves through ignorance, by following false gods and dying in futile wars. We know that much of what we do and believe will seem absurd to those who live after us. We use words such as justice and right and wrong precisely because we live in unjust ways; and we make weapons which, if they don't provoke war – and they often do – certainly make it bloodier and victory more costly. Religion offers us only more riddles – and boasts that it does so: there is no religion without mystery.

Even if we could have some reasoned understanding of what we are – some clear, positivistic explanation of the origins of our behaviour – it would not make our choices easier. Right and wrong don't exist in things the way, say, size and weight do; we have moral questions precisely because morality doesn't exist in that way. It is created in the <u>free</u> choices we make, which then become the cultural foundations of other choices. We could only have a complete understanding of our behaviour if all our choices were determined – and then of course the knowledge would be of no use to us: a puppet wouldn't be made free by learning it had strings.

None of this should make us pessimistic. The ruins of the past are also our fortress. Greek science was primitive and much of it is superseded, but its rational method remains; and the Greeks embodied this rationality in their art. The moral and dramatic arguments of the Greeks still have sharp meaning for us. Indeed, all the first creators of myths and "irrational art" were trying to use reason to understand the world; it's only their distant followers who worship the irrational for itself. Yet science must take the irrational for its blueprint and try to make utopian visions practical; and, like religion, it has its hells. Einstein said that, if he had known he would have been a clockmaker. Fortunately he didn't know; the inventor of the wheel could have said the same thing for the same reason and with as little justification.

The tragic and the rational can't be separated; free-will makes us aware of our prisons. But we create our prisons just as we create bombs and the violence of our streets; I am certain of this – violence is the product of injustice. Human behaviour isn't produced by atavistic promptings but by our cultural justifications. In the short run it is easier for governments to think otherwise, because it is easier to punish than to create justice.

Our lives are involved in small things and big things; in a private, domestic world and in the worlds of politics, technology, economics, morality. The two aspects can't be separated. It's not simply the obvious truth that, for example, changes in technology change the way we run our cities; it is even more important to understand that politics, technology, economics change the inner structure of our psychology and make us what we are. That is why we may seem to have so little choice in our daily lives. We only gain freedom <u>there</u> by accepting responsibility in the worlds of technology, economics, politics, morality – the worlds of the boundary. The way we live our ordinary, daily lives is decided by the way we live in those other worlds.

The argument that if each of us looks after his wallet god will look after the public purse, that one person may be rich without taking from others, that we can have our security at the cost of other people's vulnerability, our privilege at the cost of their deprivation, is false. The boundary does not become human – or humanize us – if we don't take responsibility for it. It is on the boundary, where our individual responsibility and initiative seem most restricted, our humanity most thinly stretched, that we find the great moral dilemmas that decide what we do in our homes.

The cup is on the table, in the house, in the street, in the city, in the nation, in the culture, in the technology....and so on; and if we go to the furthest boundary of morality, politics and art there we will find the cup on our kitchen table. If we don't accept responsibility for the boundary we lose responsibility for ourselves. We become trivialized, opportunistic and revengeful. We become objects, like the products we consume. Often that is all we are when we parade in uniforms, call for harsher punishments, buy the gutter press and talk of enterprise and freedom. Take away a yuppies feeding bowl and you have a right-wing thug.

Art helps us to understand the problem. It combines the worlds of the boundary and the world under our feet. A play may bring them together in one room, bed, family, community, institution. Then the distinction between private and public breaks down and the old solutions are seen not to work. Some writers make a fetish of the incommunication that follows. We don't need the stage to show us incommunication, we experience it in our daily life, it is the cause of anger and neglect, not the source of insight. Madmen can't make art for the same reasons they can't do science. It's not merely a question of discipline but of objective. Van Gogh didn't paint when he was mad but when he was lucid; when he was mad he mutilated and shot himself. But because human beings have struggled so long with the problems of the boundary there are now many fake mysteries – and empty slogans – to hide in. Art always apprehends the irrational rationally; it does not make a fetish of either the irrational or the rational. The worlds of the boundary and the person cannot be humanly integrated without art – without art we cannot create our humanity.

The worlds meet in Dic Edwards's plays. They create a feeling of personal responsibility and show that it is only in solving other people's problems that we have a chance to solve our own. They don't give facile, easy entertainment; instead, there is a sort of athletic tension in them, the experience of mental power and emotional daring. His recent plays, written as the political world changes, have become more "abstract" and often errupt in a sort of poetic melodrama. The language and imagery have changed in order to be more precise; the abstration remains concrete, and the melodrama is not expressionistic but analytic. The cup has not ceased to stand on the horizon.

Sometimes in a storm people count the seconds between the flash and the thunder – a very human combination of the rational and the emotional. Faced with a great scything force a vulnerable individual tries to create order and locate the danger. The experience is quite like that got from Dic Edwards's plays. They help us to understand our ordinary world by opening up the extraordinary world of our minds, and showing us how our passions and ideas are structured so surprisingly by politics, technology, morality and war. That is why his plays are important; I am a little in awe of them.

Edward Bond

Casanova Undone

(A comedy of errors)

For James Hogan

Casanova Undone was first performed at the Citizens' Theatre, Glasgow, on 26th March 1992, by the Citizens' Company. It was directed by Robert David MacDonald and the cast was as follows:

CASANOVA ....Tristram Jellinek
SOPHIE (COSTA)...Roberta Taylor
ANGELIQUE ....Siobhan Stanley

DIRECTOR...Robert David MacDonald
DESIGNER ....Kenny Miller

SET

CASANOVA's room is divided into two parts. The part that is the bed and the part that isn't.

The bed is a very big four-poster with drapes. These are kept closed most of the time. Behind them there is a world within a world. In this case a prurient world. Some way or other this world should contain the paraphernalia of sex and sexual experimentation and also things like a rhino's horn etc.

The rest of the room contains the paraphernalia of life. In this case a small table of SOPHIE's chemical apparatus; a redundant chocolate urn (redundant because there is no chocolate); CASANOVA's dressing table with its mirror. There should be a window near this mirror.

There is an exit off to the right – to another room (a bathroom) – and an exit behind the bed. This goes to a small ante-room where there is the door to the hall.

Scene One

Paris, 1790's, Casanova's room.

Late afternoon.

CASANOVA is sitting near a window. The curtains are drawn.

He is writing (his memoirs) at a desk/dressing table. There is a dressing-gown over the mirror of the dressing table.

He is very effeminate, like an old woman.

He pauses deep in thought.

Suddenly he gasps.

Casanova: That's it! That's the truth! I've found it!

[*He writes*]

[*COSTA rushes on*]

[*COSTA is a young woman dressed as a man; in fact, as a* sans culottes, *ie, in trousers and a red cap*]

[*COSTA is the woman SOPHIE*]

[*Between now and Scene Five she will be referred to as COSTA and, though a woman, as 'he'*]

[*He carries some bottles*]

[*He is breathless. He speaks pantingly*]

Costa: We're done for!

Casanova: Costa! I've discovered sublimity! I'm above ALL! I'm a god! Of a kind. [*Holds up papers*] My memoirs will ensure it! I have discovered my future!

[*COSTA collapses. He gasps and speaks indistinctly*]

Costa: Happiness is foresaken!

Casanova: What? A penis has a foreskin? Does this really need saying? You speak like a pubescent boy! Anyway, I've told you; prepuce! If we give in to all else we must not give in to vulgarity! We're not obliged to lower our standards simply because standards are lower! Think of my reputation!

Costa: [*Loudly as to a deaf man*] I said: Happiness has been condemned. They're saying it on the streets. The Committee For Public Safety have issued a decree.

Casanova: Who?

Costa: The Committee For Public Safety!

Casanova: You mean The Terror!

Costa: [*Impatiently*] Yes.

Costa: Then say it! They may murder you in hospital but it's most important that you recognise that you've been murdered rather than that you are in hospital! [*With bravado*] Say the words: The Terror!

[*COSTA takes bottles and goes to chemistry equipment. He is working on an experiment*]

Costa: The Terror has issued a decree condemning *to* DEATH all hedonists. That's seducers, fornicators...

Casanova: What are you doing?

Costa: I need to complete this experiment. It may make us rich. We must leave here as soon as possible!

Casanova: Not happy? I put up with your noxious fart-like smells thinking you are! Even though it's not good for the ambience to have our visitors constantly reminded of their bowels!

Costa: Seducers, fornicators AND sodomisers!

Casanova: Good god!

Costa: Anyone, in the end, who enjoys anything for the mere pleasure of it. You, in their eyes, Jaques, are the greatest hedonist!

Casanova: You're confusing things; there's a world of difference between happiness and 'mere pleasure'. I know because I've always sought to maximise happiness; if necessary by experiencing it myself on behalf of others in misery! And that makes me a true revolutionary, not one of your...

[*There is an explosion*]

[*CASANOVA cries out in fear*]

[*COSTA dives for cover*]

Casanova: Are you killed?

Costa: No.

Casanova: Then I'll kill you!

[*Commotion off*]

Costa: What's that? They're coming!

[*COSTA goes to bed and draws back curtain revealing its world within a world*]

[*He gets a blanket or sheet and lays it on bed and begins to put all the sexual paraphernalia in it*]

Casanova: What're you doing now?

Costa: Removing the evidence from the scene of the crime.

Casanova: What crime?

Costa: The seductions! Your pleasures!

[*CASANOVA is shocked into a momentary silence*]

Casanova: How dare you suggest that we should compromise my reputation...put those things back!

Costa: They're coming!

Casanova: They are not! That dissent, you monster, is from the neighbours! They're afraid you're going to blow them up! Stop it!

Costa: [*Talking into sheets*] You talk of doing things by proxy, but...

Casanova: Eh? Poxy?

Costa: Proxy! [*To himself*] How many times. [*Aloud*] You do it on behalf of others! You enjoy their happiness etcetera!

Casanova: Exactly!

Costa: [*With an ironical air*] Which is why, if I may say so, you are the *wisest* man in the known history of the world. BUT *nequidquam sapit qui sibi non sapit!*

Casanova: [*To audience*] A clever ploy to disarm me by using one of my own maxims! But it won't work. Put everything back!

[*COSTA pauses*]

Casanova: [*Placatory*] Consider what it means. His wisdom's vain who for himself's not wise. Are you saying that I, in this moment when I've discovered the meaning of life, should give it all up for some trifling terror? I'm as above them as they are beneath contempt!

Costa: I'm only saying that we leave Paris! For god's sake, if I were in your shoes I'd be as afraid as the wise man is of the stupid!

Casanova: You fool! They're nothing! Not even real!

Costa: You wouldn't say that if they cut your head off!

Casanova: Ha! I've cut my own head off! It's up there, way above all this apparent revolution.

Costa: Apparent?

Casanova: Well what's new about their old incorruptible morality? Death to hedonists! That's as old as time itself! The new is not made in the mirror image of the old. The new springs from the old! I am, in myself, the new and the old. So I'm an expression of revolution; a description of the very argument! I was an aristocrat now I'm not!

Costa: But are you a bourgeois?

Casanova: A bugger? Only the odd once or twice. You know that! But...

Costa: [*Loud*] A bourgeois!

Casanova: [*Refined tongue*] Of course I am! Listen to my language. How carefully I have begun to select my words. Gone all the swashbuckling verbs of my youth. When I speak I no longer use words to serve the finer – though, it has to be said, superficial – arts of word play, but to serve my own interest!

Costa: But THIS is a bourgeois revolution!

Casanova: How so?

Costa: Well all those squabbling now and chopping each others heads off! What are they? To a man: solicitors!

Casanova: You mean PETIT bourgeois! That's all YOUR revolutionaries are. They'll kill to defend freedom but what about the freedom of those they kill? Do they think they're creating a new world? Or even a new Europe? *Mais c'est moi!* I am the first European! You'll see Costa! You'll see. When my memoirs are published, they'll be a blueprint for the new politics, the new aesthetics AND the new sexuality! But how can I create my memoirs without the reputation which proves them? Replace the armory!

Costa: We must get out of here! Out of this country! I can't bear it any longer!

Casanova: D'you expect me to grovel before that claque of infertile old hens?

Costa: [*Tearfully*] They'll come for your – OUR – heads!

Casanova: On what grounds? Even if they were to say that we were a seducer...

Costa: We?!

Casanova: Don't be pedantic! They would be wrong. Because anyone CAPABLE of being a seducer, couldn't in fact be one! For in the case of such a man it's not he who seduces the woman but the woman who seduces him.

[*COSTA falls back on bed with disbelief*]

Casanova: With her beauty. She does it automatically. The whole of womanhood is predisposed to be seduced by the whole of manhood. Without her seduceability there couldn't be seduction.

Costa: But the man is the ACTIVE partner in any sex that follows so he is the one who makes the moral move!

Casanova: Clearly, in the case of seduction, he's moral but not responsible whereas she's responsible but not morally so. The end result is, *ipso facto,* there's no such thing as seducer!

Costa: What about with ugly women?

Casanova: Unseduceable!

[*Silence*]

Casanova: [*Ameliatory*] Anyway, who will find us in our little world? [*He indicates room*] Put it back.

[*COSTA begins to put things back as they were*]

[*CASANOVA returns to his writing*]

Costa: [*Sulkily*] And what about all the women who flock here?

Casanova: You will not use that word! Copulate is vulgar enough! We the bourgeois, we say: "they went to bed", "spent the night together"...We do not say...

Costa: I said 'flock!' All those women who...visit! How can your presence not be known? We're hoping that someone will come and make us rich! Isn't this what we're waiting for?

Casanova: You won't keep bringing me down to your level! We do not do it for money!

Costa: It's not an unreasonable thing for a bourgeois! And it's true, it's real. The hope is that one day we'll hit the jackpot. That in one afternoon we'll become rich enough to leave this damned city forever! But now even the rich are getting poor and countesses smell like fish-wives!

[*CASANOVA laughs*]

Costa: And that day seems further than ever away!

Casanova: You're wrong. You cannot always expect the bourgeois to be commited to what he has said should be done. The self-interest of the bourgeois is paramount. Logically, it would serve him to destroy the rest of humanity. But he has to consider: to what extent might such a holocaust impinge on that self-interest. It's a fine line.

[*COSTA is about to object*]

Casanova: Day after day, even now - at the height of the terror, duchesses, countesses, high-class ladies, come to me to experience that which made me and France great!

[*COSTA tidies bed*]

Casanova: My reputation! The memoirs would fail - be meaningless, without that reputation. Its greatness would fall victim of the most petty of all the petit bourgeoisie! Without my reputation no one would believe my memoirs! I would be nothing! Not even a mote in history's eye. No! The one great service I can give the world - my memoirs - can only be achieved by sustaining the reputation for doing what I've always done. Sweetie! Others crave immortality while I am its guarantor!

[COSTA goes to CASANOVA threateningly]

Costa: Don't call me "sweetie"!

[CASANOVA is apprehensive]

Casanova: Don't be so....

Costa: Serious? If I don't maintain 'Costa' we're done for. It's a matter of life and death! We don't chose between dildo and hell and suffering and heaven: the real choice is between life and death! If the part I act ISN'T done seriously then we're finished! In this instance, what's going on in here is more real than the sex I am. So no more "sweetie!

[There is a coded knock at the door]

Costa: *[Hurriedly preparing bed]* O, no!

Casanova: What is it?

Costa: More!

Casanova: Whore? No, no! You're not! Forgive me, I didn't mean... Listen, two days ago I wrote that man so lusts after woman that he wishes to *be* woman.

[COSTA looks at CASANOVA with incredulity]

Costa: I said!...

Casanova: Of course, our reactionary ethics demand that men should be men which is why we have the obnoxious posturing of men as warriors! War is merely a gesture by man to deny the woman in him. Only a man is more woman than man can be lover enough to know a woman's needs. If you are a whore then so am I!

[Pause]

Costa: I said there's someone at the door!

Casanova: Door?

Costa: The knock!

Casanova: A patron? Then let her in! She will be made deliquescent by degrees!

Costa: [*To himself*] To the knees!

[*COSTA closes curtains around bed and goes off around back of bed*]

[*After a moment, some talking is heard off, behind the bed*]

[*COSTA comes on*]

Casanova: Well?

Costa: A duchess I think. She's dark and old. Says she's from Lybia.

Casanova: Sores on her labia? But how do you know? We must not be poxed!

Costa: [*Very impatient*] I said she says she's from Lybia! Why don't you use your trumpet? I'm suffering beyond what's reasonable! D'you enjoy living with this factorised sense?

Casanova: Why're you swearing at me? Calm yourself!

[*Pause*]

Casanova: Prepare her!

[*COSTA goes off behind bed*]

[*The light begins to fade*]

[*CASANOVA pours himself a glass of wine*]

[*He takes the covering from the mirror of the dressing table*]

[*He drinks*]

Casanova: Scopolo wine!

[*He touches up his make-up; adjusts his wig etc*]

[*There are noises off which CASANOVA doesn't hear - Some mumbling and giggling; even a little stumbling and finally a body flopping on the bed*]

Casanova: [*Into the mirror*] Light dying. Doesn't seem right: light dying in Paris. [*Pause*] How dying light adds youth! [*Pause*] 20! Went to the greatest ball there ever was. The Clipped Yew. Everyone went as a tree! [*Laughs*] Ball for the marriage of the young dauphin. [*Pause. Laughs to himself*] Made love to the beautiful sex-pot Presidente Portail! Thought I was the king! We all wore big trees on our heads. Easy to pretend to be the king with a tree on your head. Anyway, weren't we all kings? That bastard was a such horny seducer every whore in Paris had come to try her luck! He was in such a disguise no one could recognise him! When the king's unrecognisable all his courtiers are kings! [*Laughs*] And I had the one and only queen: The Presidente Portail. [*Laughs again, controlling himself with difficulty*] She was not pleased when, returning with me from the most HEATED fucking, she saw the king - who'd taken of his headdress, talking with Madame Etoiles! Who was wet to her ankles. [*Laughs quietly*] See how I've changed? Wouldn't do that now. I'd find all that stuff on my head too restricting!

[*COSTA comes up close to CASANOVA and speaks in his ear*]

[*Sighs come from behind the curtain*]

Costa: She's ready Jaques.

Casanova: Ready? So quickly?

Costa: I told you. She's old.

[*CASANOVA sighs*]

Costa: She was soon overcome by the opiate. She seemed more intrigued than is usual that I was preparing her for you.

[*Pause*]

Casanova: Is there a confusion here? You sound as if you expect ME... I hate foreplay. You know that! It's for the petty seducer. The hedonist. But when we talk about the maximising of happiness, that's a different thing.

[*Silence*]

Costa: I don't want to do it.

Casanova: What?

Costa: I've seen enough of breasts that fall to the waist like empty sails and thighs that hang like monstrous foreskins.

[*CASANOVA laughs*]

Casanova: Prepuce I said! Ha, ha.

Costa: I mean it Jaques! This woman is uglier than an act of violence...

Casanova: Nonsense! *Sublata lucerna nullum discrimen inter feminas!* When the lamp is taken away all women look alike; something I paraphrased from St. Augustine you will remember? Look into the street: it's getting dark!

[*COSTA sighs deeply*]

[*He quickly puts on some make-up*]

[*He ties a stomach around his waist and puts padding in the crotch of his trousers*]

[*COSTA takes CASANOVA'S wig and puts it on*]

[*He takes a house-coat of CASANOVA'S and puts that on*]

[*He picks up dildo on way*]

[*He goes behind curtain*]

Casanova: Go to it! I am immortalised by my juices! ha, ha!

[*Pause*]

[*CASANOVA looks as though he's had a revelation*]

Casanova: [*To audience*]   When I let Costa do it, it's so that I can sublimate my sexuality! This is what I've discovered! Now I understand!

[*CASANOVA picks up his pen and prepares himself over his paper*]

Casanova: [*To curtain in a raised whisper*]   I am ready! [*Pause. To audience*] Yes! I'm able, when necessary, to sublimate my sexuality so that it becomes wisdom! And this is the proof! I can enjoy an enhanced reputation – necessary for the credibility of my memoirs – while someone else does the dirty work. I mean, the 'practical' work! What could be wiser?! I must write that down!

[*COSTA throws wig out*]

[*There are sighs from behind the curtain*]

[*CASANOVA writes*]

Casanova: [*Looking up*]   And besides, I simply don't have the time with all this writing to do!

[*There are great sighs*]

[*CASANOVA picks up wig and puts it on*]

[*Lights down*]

[*In between scenes there is a blue light*]

[*In the blue light we see COSTA leave bed and CASANOVA get into it*]

[*The woman in bed is the ANGELIQUE actress with a mask on. But we only anyway see her in the blue light*]

Scene Two

[*Morning*]

[*COSTA is in chair, still wearing CASANOVA's 'housecoat'*]

Casanova: [*From behind curtain*] Don't be so palpable sweet! Why so sentimental about parting? Togetherness is only an apparition. Like life. It may not even be me you're looking at now! Come again O fair Lybian with your eyes of topaz!

[*While CASANOVA speaks, COSTA gets up from chair. He sees his* sans cullottes *cap and puts it on*]

[*He looks in mirror*]

[*He breathes in proudly*]

[*His pride quickly turns to sadness*]

Costa: [*Into mirror*] I am not!

[*He takes off cap and angrily throws it. He looks closely into mirror examining his make-up with an almost fatalistic air*]

[*CASANOVA's head appears through curtain. His wig is askew*]

Casanova: Costa?

[*COSTA turns to him*]

[*CASANOVA throws dildo to floor*]

Casanova: I'm forever clearing up after you. It's very depressing!

[*COSTA takes dildo, goes off and returns*]

[*CASANOVA sits on the edge of the bed. He looks terribly jaded*]

[*COSTA suddenly snatches CASANOVA's wig and puts it petulantly on his own head. He looks in mirror*]

Casanova: You seem disgruntled Costa.

Costa: The whole thing IS a sham.

Casanova: Don't be so petty! You should subordinate your will to the fine service you give, just as I sublimate mine! Besides, you know it's a delightful idea that they go to bed with only an apparent Casanova but wake up with the real! It's not dishonest to experience by proxy the joy others would be experiencing if they weren't miserable, so why should this be dishonest? It serves a greater goal!

Costa: I don't mean that! I mean it's not worth it! We're putting ourselves in danger for a few sous!

Casanova: The bourgeois will always put his life in danger for a few sous!

Costa: I'm talking about yesterday's decree. They're coming for the hedonists. Even you said that the hedonist is only a petty lover who indulges in foreplay.

Casanova: Exactly!

Costa: But that's me!

Casanova: [*Shocked*] You!

Costa: Preparing your way!

Casanova: But dearest child you haven't told me this before! You mean you actually derive a pleasure from your fumblings with these old maids?

Costa: No!

Casanova: O well. There you are then, you can't be a hedonist!

Costa: But THEY don't know it! The Committee!

Casanova: The mirror, please!

[*COSTA covers the mirror*]

[*CASANOVA comes to his chair and flops in it very tiredly*]

[*COSTA goes off*]

[*Bach's Violin Sonata No. 1 in G minor (BWV 1001) can be heard off*]

Casanova: [*Lifts himself a little*] That music! What is it? [*He puts his trumpet to his ear*] Such sublime music! Like a voice crying in the wilderness. Costa! That music! Can you hear it?

Costa: [*Off. Shouting*] No!

Casanova: No?

Costa: [*Off*] It must be in your mind. It often happens with deafness. An inner music.

Casanova: [*Serenely*] But if it's in my mind it must be my mind making it up!

[*COSTA comes back on*]

Casanova: Costa! D'you think I may be a great composer and not even know it?

Costa: No.

Casanova: Why not?

Costa: Because now I can hear it.

Casanova: [*Petulantly*] You heard it all along!

Costa: I was hoping it would go away.

Costa: Why?

Casanova: Because it's probably some urchin after the few sous we have.

Casanova: Whoever is playing that violin inhabits a world where none of the base senses have currency and that's a man for me. Go out and enquire politely whether he might not like to step inside and play for the Chevalier de Seingalt, knight of the Golden Spur, a partita or two.

Costa: I thought you were a bourgeois!

Casanova: Do you think the bourgeois could exist without reference to what went before him? Even a child at his father's funeral knows instinctively that though you bury the machine of his creation you don't bury the patent. Nothing, not even a thing as desirable as a bourgeois millenium, just falls from the sky. Out!

[COSTA goes gruffly. After a moment he returns. The music is still playing]

Casanova: Well?

[Pause]

Casanova: Costa!

Costa: It's a young lady.

Casanova: Young lady? What do you mean?

Costa: Well... how can I explain?...

Casanova: Don't be ironic; it's cruel.

Costa: I'll send her away.

Casanova: Why?!

Costa: I don't think we should pursue this.

Casanova: Pursue what? What is it? What's going on? Young lady? Don't tell me you're jealous!

Costa: *[Incredulosuly]* What?!

[CASANOVA is suddenly at sixes and sevens not knowing what to do]

[He puts on dressing gown]

Costa: We don't know why she's here.

Casanova: Because she knows that I'm here!

Costa: If that's the case that should concern us.

Costa: *[Severely]* Get her in? You may learn something about aesthetics!

[COSTA goes off gasping]

[CASANOVA hurriedly places a footstool before his chair.

[The music stops]

[COSTA comes on with ANGELIQUE who is carrying a violin]

[ANGELIQUE looks perplexed. She is looking closely at COSTA as she comes into the room]

Angelique: *[To COSTA]* But...

[COSTA puts a finger to his lips and indicates CASANOVA reverentially]

[CASANOVA, with best face, holds out an arm to welcome ANGELIQUE to him]

[ANGELIQUE goes to CASANOVA]

Costa: *[Man's voice]* Mademoiselle Angelique.

Casanova: Of course! Angel!

[COSTA goes off behind bed but can be seen looking on]

Casanova: Tell me; what is it you were playing!

Angelique: It was the Sonata Number One in G Minor by Bach.

Casanova: Beautiful!

Angelique: It's unpublished.

Casanova: [*Gasping. Horror*] What!

Angelique: It's from a set of six. I've seen the original manuscript. It's in Bach's own calligraphic hand. He was so masterful. It's as if the words and notes themselves play out. You feel that anything he touched would turn to music. In the beautiful script he's written; *sei solo a violin senza basso accompagnato.*

Casanova: I am Italian!

Angelique: I love the Italians. They're so cultured.

Casanova: But you speak Italian. YOU are cultured! Such an intellect!... Tell me; you say these pieces are unpublished?

Angelique: Yes. I have a handwritten copy.

Casanova: But what are you holding back from the world? In what I heard I could see such a universe of inventiveness. From one violin an orchestra of instruments. Around the melody of a single instrument, two, three, four voices moving contrapuntally.

Angelique: [*Surprised*] You know!

Casanova: Know? Of course I know! I can still hear the echoes. How is it done? How does one create the illusion of a melody accompanied by a bass? How does one create the illusion of harmony embedded in a single horizontal line?

Angelique: You DO know!

[*CASANOVA suddenly falls to his knees before her*]

[*ANGELIQUE looks around worriedly*]

[*COSTA puts his hands over his eyes for fear of looking*]

Casanova: Of course I know my child my sweet. I am a slave of beauty.

[*CASANOVA's bald head is in ANGELIQUE's lap. Her face grimaces*]

Casanova: Even the feet! What I DO know is that the performer, the violinist, must penetrate more deeply than mere technique will allow. Isn't it true? Must he not clarify the implied harmonies and the pseudo-polyphony? Must he not separate the melody from the accompanying bass?

[*He kisses her knees*]

[*She gasps*]

Casanova: And particularly in the fugal movements, must he not bring out the subject which is often embedded in the lower strings?

[*He puts a hand between her legs*]

[*She suddenly cries out and jumps up pushing him off*]

Angelique: Who d'you think you are?!

[*He falls backwards to the floor*]

[*COSTA's face goes*]

[*CASANOVA grunts incoherently*]

[*ANGELIQUE rushes off to look for COSTA*]

[*CASANOVA gets up*]

[*He puts his hands to his head in distress and realises he doesn't have his wig on*]

Casanova: My Wig! Ruined for a wig! Costa!

[*COSTA rushes on*]

Casanova: Costa! Do you realise what's happened? You're wearing my wig and it's cost me my reputation! It must be redeemed!

Costa: That's easy enough.

[*He takes off wig and hands it to CASANOVA*]

Casanova: Not that! My reputation!

Costa: But surely there's no need to make such a fuss. Just this afternoon you said that the man doesn't seduce the woman and you've shown you were right. You didn't seduce her!

Casanova: Don't play games with me! Get after that girl!

[*COSTA laughs uncontrollably*]

[*CASANOVA suddenly rushes to bed and takes sword quickly from its scabbard and holds it to COSTA's throat*]

[*Both are suddenly very serious*]

[*CASANOVA is even tearful*]

Casanova: Don't...mock me!

Costa: I wasn't!

Casanova: Then why'd you laugh?

Costa: Not you...just the picture...it looked funny.

Casanova: When you die you can laugh at your life but while I live you prepare your tears for mine. Get the girl and bring her back. This business isn't finished.

[*COSTA decorously takes CASANOVA's wig from his head and places it on his own*]

[*COSTA goes*]

[*CASANOVA sees himself in the mirror. He suddenly lashes out with his sword*]

Casanova: [*Defiantly*] *Carpe diem!*

[*CASANOVA sits*]

[*COSTA returns with ANGELIQUE but she remains at the back side of the bed and won't come further into the room*]

Angelique: [*Sotto voce*] I told you, Monsieur, I came to see you not your mother!

[*COSTA gestures for her to be quiet*]

Angelique: [*Desparately*] My mistress needs your help! She says that you are the only person who can help her! It's a matter of life and death! And now that I've seen you I understand her: you look so much younger than you should! You can do it! You must please help us!

[*COSTA is perplexed*]

Costa: [*Man's voice*] Your mistress is who?

Angelique: Madame d'Urfé. Do you remember her?

[*Pause*]

Costa: You must come back here tomorrow.

[*ANGELIQUE looks at CASANOVA who has become aware of her presence*]

Angelique: Tomorrow? But I....

Costa: [*Mock anger*] You weren't expecting me to come with you? Now?

[*Pause*]

Costa: It's absurd. Do you have any idea how dangerous the streets are for me? Come tomorrow!

[*He suddenly takes her roughly*]

[*He gives her a perfunctory kiss*]

[*She gasps*]

Costa: Tell your mistress nothing. If you speak a word of any of it to her or to anyone, I won't help. And I'll know if you do.

Angelique: You... You must help!

[*ANGELIQUE goes*]

[*COSTA comes back on*]

[*He takes the wig off and dumps it on CASANOVA's head*]

Costa: I think she's an agent of The Terror.

Casanova: What? What do you mean?

Costa: A spy! I think she's a spy!

Casanova: But if you thought that why'd you let her go?

Costa: If I hadn't someone would have come for her!

Casanova: If she was a spy she would have come in disguise. She was too real!

Costa: She was a spy! She should have been in awe of our reputation and she wasn't!

Casanova: "Our"?!

Costa: Yours! Mine! It doesn't matter. She believed one of us was you. In fact, she believed I was you! When I let her in she addressed me as Monsieur Casanova.

Casanova: You mean she found me and didn't know it was me? This is an outrage!

Costa: It'll be more of an outrage if she informs on us!

Casanova: We can prevent it! She must be seduced!

[*Pause*]

Costa: Do you mean in this case that you will do it or that I will as though I were you? Because if the latter....

Casanova: She thinks you're me! You must do it!

Costa: This is madness! We should get out of here now! I don't want to see her again. I have a feeling that if I do she'll be at the head of a band of *sans cullottes.*

Casanova: I want that girl seduced!

Costa: But she didn't come to be seduced!

Casanova: Nonsense! All women want to be seduced. That's why they seduce men. You know I'm right.

Costa: This young woman doesn't want to be seduced!

Casanova: How'd you know?

Costa: I know. [*Pause*] I know!

Casanova: I see. And what about all your Duchesses and Countesses: that random drift of noble slags in and out of here?

Costa: But they come to be engaged with! That's all. And I'm certainly not seducing them.

Casanova: Of course not! They're unseduceable! They've been through it so many times they've forgotten the meaning of the word!

Costa: But if I WERE required to seduce them - or her - I couldn't do it! I'm not a seducer! That's the difference between a real seducer and a pretend one. I can't do it!

Casanova: You'll do it! I want that girl done!

[*Pause*]

Costa: Very well! Suppose I do it! If I, as YOU, actually seduce her, that ACTUALLY means that I have seduced her. When she finds out, as she will, that I am not you but that you are you, she will be outraged because she has already rejected you: albeit it wiglessly and therefore unjustly....

Casanova: [*Holding back his outrage*] *Nequidquam sapit qui sibi non sapit!*

[*COSTA flinches*]

Casanova: If Madameoiselle Angelique thinks you're me then she hasn't rejected me! That's all that matters!

Costa: But you said she came to be seduced by you. Not me. So she will have been seduced by someone who is not you when she wouldn't have wanted to be by someone who is you! You! Because she rejected....

Casanova: Shut this bollocks up! In the end, once she's been seduced, she'll be grateful for it. I know better than you. In fact, I know better than any woman!

Costa: Perhaps because you've taken on certain of the attributes of womanhood.

Casanova: What d'you mean?

Costa: She thought you were my mother!

[*CASANOVA lets out a cry of outrage*]

Casanova: How can you speak so perversely when we're considering the seduction of a young and beautiful woman!

[*CASANOVA's anger quickly turns into the sobbing of an old woman*]

Costa: [*Bitterly*] Anyway, she will have been seduced by me!

Casanova: [*Over his sobbing*] That's what I want to hear! Let it be that I'm immortalised by YOUR juices; or anyway your lubricants! What difference do you think THAT would make historically? None! How often was the work of a great Rennaissance painter like Michaelangelo actually carried out by a minion? VERY often!

[*Pause*]

Costa: Very well then. And what if you're right? What if she's not a spy? And what if she's come to be...to seduce the great Casanova and I succeed and in the process, fall in love with her?

Casanova: How dare you suggest that you may fall in love with a woman! Particularly someone you've seduced! The idea is repugnant! The whole point of seduction is conquest! To get to the top of the mountain without slipping on the snow! Furthermore, you have no right to suggest that in seducing this woman you might betray me when it's me you're seducing her for! You will seduce her Costa and stop this fucking whingeing!

Costa: If I were to fall in love with her, where then do you think we'd be? We would have no money coming in because I would refuse to share my new love with the dying whims of old reactionary hags!

Casanova: THAT is a reactionary idea! Let's get this straight: the bourgeoisie do NOT fall in love! The nearest they get to it is with sentimentalism which is the exploitation of emotion for the greater good of the bourgeois cause. It's only a posture towards love made plausible by great handfuls of good manners. It's not possible that by day you could be the lackey of this petit bourgeois Terror in your trousers and red cap and by night great warrior in the real revolution - in my bed - and not see which is the greater cause! You've lived too long with me and learned too much to be stupid. Tomorrow we will take her!

[*Silence*]

Costa: [*To audience*] I won't do it! [*To CASANOVA*] Very well, I'll do it.

[*Lights down*]

[*In the blue light we see COSTA take a small bottle from his collection of bottles and keep it in hand*]

[*COSTA holds the bottle up, crosses himself and says a prayer*]

Scene Three

Late afternoon

CASANOVA is wigless in his chair.

He is asleep.

Around the bed area is dark; near CASANOVA there is more light.

COSTA is bent over CASANOVA listening for his breathing.

COSTA is dressed as san culottes.

COSTA holds up a small bottle checking on its emptiness.

He puts it amongst his bottles.

There is a coded knock.

COSTA goes.

A moment later, ANGELIQUE rushes on.

Costa: I just want you to know the truth!

[ANGELIQUE stops near bed and turns towards COSTA then turns away again. She is agitated]

Angelique: And I feel just the same!

[ANGELIQUE speaks almost without punctuation]

[COSTA is unable to get a word in]

Angelique: I need to tell you about my mistress! You may recall much about her yourself. But you wouldn't know she saved my life when she took me in as a child. Now I have the opportunity to save her's. I would do anything to be able to do that! I would even recreate who I am; give myself up entirely for the greater good; my mistress's cause, knowing that I would win myself back in the hour of our success!

She knew you would let me in yesterday. She said she never knew anyone more sensitive to music. She said it's as if you've always known how to speak for humanity when humanity must be silent. She taught me to play. Well she made me enthusiastic; then she paid for my lessons. Now I play in her service. If it would save her life I would play music to the death! I'm not an aesthetic person. I don't think a thing is made necessarily good by its being beautiful. It must have some other use. It must be true of you: that you'll be moved as though my lady's plight were the saddest partita, saying the things that she dare not speak.

[By now ANGELIQUE has reached CASANOVA and the light]

Costa: But it wasn't me you spoke to about the music.

[She suddenly sees CASANOVA and gasps]

[She turns to COSTA who stand in silence looking at her]

[She looks back at CASANOVA then to COSTA]

Angelique: No! You can't be him! *[About the way he's dressed]* I can see now you're...

[COSTA nods negatively]

Angelique: You're too young.

[ANGELIQUE looks to CASANOVA and realises her error. She looks to COSTA for confirmation of what she suspects and he nods affirmatively]

Angelique: Mother?

[COSTA nods affirmatively and mouths the word: 'Mother']

Angelique: O, but he won't be able to do it! Look at him sleeping and it's not even dark! He won't be able to do it!

Costa: Do what?

Angelique: Carry out my lady's plan! She's prepared to give her whole fortune to it! And he won't be able to do it!

[*Pause*]

Costa: Fortune?

Angelique: Yes! All of it!

Costa: What exactly do you mean, fortune?

Angelique: Her fortune! Her wealth!

Costa: How...how much is that?

Angelique: I don't know...exactly. But it was enough to make her fear she might lose it to the *sans cullottes.* It's in the East. In the safe-keeping of a Count Waldstein of Dux.

Costa: Dux?

Angelique: It's a town in Bohemia.

Costa: Bohemia!

[*COSTA is awe-struck*]

Angelique: Yes!

Costa: I've heard of Bohemia! Isn't it beautiful? Isn't it overrun with great endless forests in which a man may be lost forever?

Angelique: The castle of Dux is right in the middle of such a forest.

Costa: [*To audience*] If lux means light could Dux mean dark? Like a great cloak in which to wrap ourselves? And with money enough that we will never need to leave our dark for this dying light! We must go to Dux! [*To ANGELIQUE*] And this Count...what was his name?

Angelique: Waldstein.

Costa: [*Feverishly; holding on to ANGELIQUE*] You must tell me: what is it your mistress wants?

Angelique: But...what difference could it make now?

Costa: You said: to save her life you would do anything. You can at least tell your story.

[*Pause*]

Angelique: My mistress is the sweetest saint but she is VERY ugly. She is so ugly the mere sight of her terrorises people. Consequently she wears a veil. All the time. I suppose it may be a reason for my rejection of beauty as a philosophy in itself. Anyway, SHE reasons that her ugliness must be a prelude to death. But she doesn't want to die! Then she heard of this great magician who may be able to help her...his name was Saint Germain...and so she went to see him. Unfortunately, he was himself about to die but he did say that he knew of only one way to avoid death and that was to be reborn...

Costa: Reborn?

Angelique: Yes! And he said that there was only one man who could help her; who could do the thing that needs to be done. [*Pause*] Monsieur Casanova. SHE knew it could be done by him because she'd had experience of him many years before at the Ball Of The Clipped Yew when she'd posed as the magnificently beautiful Presidente Portail. She had worn a mask, of course. Monsieur Casanova had pretended to be the king in order to woo the Presidente Portail. Well, he won my mistress in his mask while she wore her's. Later, the king unmasked and she pretended to be furious as though she'd been duped!

Costa: I know that story! SHE was the Presidente Portail?

Angelique: Yes.

[*Silence*]

Costa: But what it is she wants done?

Angelique: I don't think it can be. Now that I've seen him. Age IS so terrible.

Costa: Angelique! Monsieur Casanova has powers which may yet startle the world. Tell me!

[*Silence*]

Angelique: The magician told her that...that on a certain night, when the moon is in a particular phase, and with the appropriate magic, if my mistress were impregnated, she would conceive and give birth to a boy child. During the birth she would inhabit the body of the child and be rid of her old carcass.

[*Silence*]

[*COSTA turns away from ANGELIQUE deep in thought*]

Costa: How ugly is she?

Angelique: I don't...but no more ugly than Monsieur Casanova!

Costa: You say she wears a veil?

Angelique: Always.

[*Silence*]

Costa: [*Severely*] It can be done. He can do it.

Angelique: But how?

Costa: He's a magician! [*Indicates bottles etc.*] I've seen him make

gold of base metals. And here, in this room, I've seen him double
the quantity of mercury – a very expensive metal...

Angelique: Yes, but that's...I mean that's a different thing from...from
this!

[*Silence*]

Costa: There's a way that we can help to ensure success.

Angelique: What is it?

Costa: How determined are you?

Angelique: I told you. If necessary I would die for her.

Costa: D'you think you could trust me?

Angelique: Well...there IS my mistress's fortune.

[*Pause*]

Costa: We have to make him confident.

Angelique: Yes?

Costa: I mean UTTERLY...DEEPLY confident.

Angelique: Very well.

Costa: We need to use a little magic. You see...in human
relationships, in success or the achievement of endeavour,
confidence is always needed and magic is always used to achieve
it. Confidence is made of magic.

Angelique: Magic?

Costa: Legerdemain.

[*COSTA attempts a little magical trick with his hands but it doesn't work*]

Angelique: What was that?

Costa: I was...um...just demonstrating the principles of my argument.

[*Pause*]

Costa: I'm a little...excited. That's all.

Angelique: I'm sure you could have done it!

[*Pause*]

Costa: We must get him into the bed! When he wakes, you'll be
beside him and he'll believe he's just given you your happiest
night!

Angelique: Monsieur!

Costa: That's what you'll tell him.

Angelique: But...you want me to take my clothes off ?

Costa: Well...we have to make him believe!

Angelique: But!...

[*COSTA holds ANGELIQUE's face*]

Costa: Mademoiselle Angelique, don't be afraid!

Angelique: But I don't understand! He'll know that he didn't go to bed with me! That we didn't kiss! That we didn't...you know...

Costa: Pet? Foreplay?

Angelique: Yes.

Costa: O, he sleeps very heavily. He won't even know how long he's been asleep! Nor will he care! He IS a great magician. Daily, I tell you, duchesses, marquises...even, I've seen it, some women from the Convention, come here and he...I don't know...He's able to make of this room what it's not! It's as if it becomes a theatre and they're not only the audience but also the actors! If I may be blunt: Monsieur Casanova's whole reputation is rooted in this phenomenon: that while others – lesser lovers and all mortals, struggle to achieve climax, Casanova has climax, as it were, put at his disposal. Climax, in the case of Casanova, is a concept created by his reputation rather than the reward of a lover's perserverance.

[*Silence*]

Angelique: [*Alarmed*] But does that mean...?

[*Pause*]

Costa: Yes?

Angelique: Does that mean he doesn't do it?

Costa: It means he doesn't have to do it.

Angelique: But then...he wouldn't have done it!

Costa: But it would have been done!

Angelique: How?!

Costa: Magic!

[*Pause*]

Angelique: Are you speaking metaphorically?

Costa: It's an area too profound for aesthetics.

Angelique: Then I'm not happy!

Costa: Why?

Angelique: Because...because it doesn't make sense to me! If he doesn't do it, how is it done? A woman would know.

[*Silence*]

Costa: I do it.

Angelique: You?!

Costa: Yes! You see, for Casanova to retain his powers his reputation must be constantly renewed. But implied in that reputation is that he has a more...philosophical role than would be the case with men of lesser reputation. In other words to enhance the reputation it's absolutely necessary that he does less of what it is that makes the reputation enhanced. And in that respect I am charged by duty - as minion to this master - to... serve.

[*Silence*]

Costa: [*Indicating CASANOVA*] Shall we?

Angelique: Yes.

[*They struggle with CASANOVA*]

[*CASANOVA snores through this*]

[*COSTA puts CASANOVA'S wig on CASANOVA. This causes ANGELIQUE to laugh*]

[*In attempting to stop her, COSTA and ANGELIQUE accidentally meet and touch over the body of CASANOVA*]

[*COSTA turns away with an apology*]

Costa: I'm sorry.

Angelique: Why?

[*Silence*]

[*ANGELIQUE moves towards COSTA over the body of CASANOVA*]

[*She touches COSTA's face with her hand*]

[*Slowly, she brings COSTA to her and kisses him passionately, still over the body of CASANOVA*]

[*ANGELIQUE takes her clothes off*]

[*CASANOVA groans loudly objecting to the activity over his body*]

[*ANGELIQUE gets into bed*]

[*COSTA goes from bed*]

[*Silence*]

Angelique: You wonder why I did that? [*Pause*] Now I feel safe.

Costa: When he wakes we'll say nothing of your mistress.

Angelique: No?

Costa: To convince him of the integrity of the plan we would have to tell him about the night he spent with your mistress. But he's always thought that he spent that night with the Presidente Portail! He would be very disappointed to learn the truth. To the point that...

Angelique: O, I understand!

Costa: As it is, we may have to dupe him a little. To make him believe he's with someone else other than your mistress.

Casanova: [*Waking*] Costa!

[*COSTA indicates to ANGELIQUE to do her bit*]

[*COSTA comes forwards to audience looking worried and wringing his hands*]

[*COSTA goes*]

Casanova: [*Sitting up bewilderedly*] Costa! Where....

[*He sees ANGELIQUE*]

Casanova: You! Then...

[*Pause*]

Angelique: [*Smiling*] It's done. And never better.

[*She strokes his chest*]

Casanova: You were?...

Angelique: Overcome.

Casanova: So must I have been! I can't remember a thing!

Angelique: You can make ecstacy of a whisper. It's a kind of magic.

[*Pause*]

Casanova: But surely, in this state of ecstacy, it's difficult to distinguish something that's ACTUALLY happening from something only SEEMING to happen.

Angelique: It happened! But YOU know it happened!

Casanova: Of course it happened. Forgive me for seeming to doubt. It's simply that, as a student of the body I have a predisposition to anatomise. In this case, your ecstacy. For example, was it ecstatic to the point that you may have been unable to distinguish whether it was *I* who did it or some godly incubus?

Angelique: O, it was a god, it was you! I have your face painted on my eyes.

Casanova: Then it *is* done!

Costa: Hear, hear to that!

[*CASANOVA gasps with outrage*]

Casanova: Costa! What d'you mean I hurt her twat? I won't have it! A day will come when the bourgeoisie will so rebel against that kind of language that they'll abandon any act that may be commented upon so disgustingly! [*About ANGELIQUE*] Look at the face. There is no trace of pain!

[*ANGELIQUE suppresses a laugh*]

[*COSTA sighs*]

Casanova: You see? She is happy!

[*COSTA fetches CASANOVA's ear-trumpet*]

[*He puts it to his ear*]

[*ANGELIQUE looks dismayed*]

Costa: [*Shouting into trumpet*] And I said I'm happy for you!

Casanova: [*Angrily*] Costa!

[*Pause*]

Casanova: [*Happily*] Well I'm happy too! And you sweet?

Angelique: Very happy! The night has been a thousand journeys!

Casanova: *Nolo nimis facilem difficilemque nimis!*

Angelique: What's that?

Casanova: It's something I paraphrased from Saint Paul: I want a woman neither to give in too easily nor to resist too much!

[*Laughter*]

[*COSTA prepares a bowl of water for washing*]

[*CASANOVA gropes at ANGELIQUE beneath the bed-clothes*]

[*ANGELIQUE pushes him off good-humouredly*]

Angelique: Now, now, monsieur...

Casanova: Call me Jaques, please! I think you can say we have undone etiquette!

Angelique: What was it you said? *Nolo nolo...*

Casanova: Yes, *nimis facilem....*

[*ANGELIQUE begins to get out of bed*]

Angelique: I'm sorry Monsieur Jaques, I must go.

Casanova: So soon?

Angelique: I have things to do.

Casanova: Violin practise?

Angelique: Well yes, as a matter of fact.

[*ANGELIQUE is sitting on the rear edge of bed*]

Casanova: My sweet! One thing please! Let me have one...Costa, avert your eyes...one look at your behind. So that if I die tonight, it may carry me to heaven!

Angelique: But...

Casanova: Angelique! You have seen, no doubt, Boucher's *L'Odelisque?*

Angelique: Yes.

Casanova: A work of art?

Angelique: They say so.

Casanova: Why?

Angelique: I...I don't know.

Casanova: Because it was revolutionary! It was a painting, essentially, of a woman's bum! And I was the discoverer of that beautiful creation which she carried through the first part of her life but which carried her thereafter: once it had been revealed. For it belonged to Madameoiselle Louison, a young woman I found working in a hotel. Her arse gave ultimate meaning to her life. In fact, to my life too. And though she had no family name she had this bum like a brace of lily bulbs. Please Mademoiselle... Costa, curtain! Who knows what I may not see in your charming rump? Perhaps a revival of the whole of French culture!

[COSTA draws curtains]

[CASANOVA gasps from behind curtain]

Casanova: M-m-m-m, yes!

[COSTA peeps through curtains]

[He looks back out with something like longing]

Casanova: You know since Boucher did his arse everyone's doing them. More arses have been painted in France in the last twenty years than in the previous history of the world! And all because of me.

[Laughter]

[COSTA paces then sits with his head in his hands]

Casanova: [From behind curtain] You may or may not be pleased to know, Angelique, that in my life I have spent nights on pillows of bums!

Angelique: [From behind curtain; laughing] Monsieur Jaques. You are funny!

Casanova: [From behind curtain] I'm a humanist! And what a wonderful, human development in the history of art that man in all the highest places worships now what even the pauper has hitherto only sat on: the bum!

[ANGEIQUE laughs but suddenly breaks off]

Casanova: Ah! I could go happily to my death now that I've born witness! [Mock tragic] And now you're going!

[ANGELIQUE comes from behind curtain of bed]

[She comes quickly to COSTA and kisses him]

[COSTA is reluctant]

Angelique: [*Sotto voce*] I'm afraid.

Costa: Of what?

Angelique: He won't be able to do it. I saw his...

Costa: Penis?

Angelique: Yes.

Costa: Listen, if you knew the life of that...that...root...

Angelique: No wait! I saw him.

Costa: You saw him?

Angelique: He was trying to....

[*ANGELIQUE mimics a masturbatory action*]

Costa: Masturbate?

Angelique: Well yes. Over my behind. But he couldn't get an erection!

Costa: Don't worry! We have the magic...!

Angelique: But why should I believe that? The magic was supposed to give him confidence! If he's not confident over my so-called work of art how will he be confident over my ugly mistress? I don't think we can do it! I'm afraid!

Costa: But Angelique! He's...he's...well he IS old. Older than he was. I mean...just after waking he's an ordinary man. But given time to prepare he can produce any amount of unexpected...

Angelique: I know what you're doing. I can understand. I know you love him and...

Costa: Love him?

Angelique: Well like I love my mistress! But I just don't know!

[*COSTA turns to audience*]

Costa: [*To audience*] It'll have to be the meal! [*To ANGELIQUE*] Angelique, listen, if I can show you in some other way, just what powers he has will it be enough?

Angelique: But how?

Costa: Well... supposing we invite you here for a meal?

Angelique: A Meal?

Costa: Yes! Don't you see? There is no food in Paris!

Angelique: If there's no food, how can we have a meal?

Costa: Precisely! He will conjure it up for you! NOT just a meal. Something incomparable even for easier times. You would have to agree that he's far more likely to be able to impregnate your mistress than to conjure up a meal in Paris in these days. He will feed you and when he does there'll be proof enough that we can succeed.

[*Pause*]

Angelique: Worse than him not doing it would be for my mistress to believe he will, only then to discover he can't! It would be like discovering that god was dead!

Costa: Trust me!

[*ANGELIQUE kisses COSTA but both are hesitant*]

Angelique: What is it?

Costa: Nothing.

Casanova: [*From behind curtain*] Costa! Has Angelique gone yet?

Costa: This minute. I was wondering my lord, whether it might not be a good idea, that we, I mean, of course, you, don't invite Mademoiselle Angelique to join us tomorrow for dinner. I'm sure we can present a menu that's quite special.

Casanova: That's a splendid idea!

[*ANGELIQUE shows surprise at CASANOVA's readiness to agree to something that seems impossible*]

[*COSTA holds out his arms to ANGELIQUE as if to say: "You see?"*]

[*ANGELIQUE smiles weakly*]

[*As ANGELIQUE and COSTA go off, CASANOVA opens curtains*]

[*COSTA returns excitedly*]

Costa: Jaques!..

Casanova: What's this about a meal?

Costa: How could you have so readily agreed to a meal when you know that there's so little food in Paris?!

Casanova: Does that matter?

Costa: What do you mean?

Casanova: I mean: who needs food to create a meal!

Costa: What?!

Casanova: Costa! If you need food to enjoy a meal, you're mundane and REACTIONARY.

[*From this point COSTA washes CASANOVA after first getting him out of bed*]

[*He begins by washing his face and then works down*]

[*When it comes to his behind, CASANOVA bends forward and COSTA lifts his night-shirt*]

Costa: Ah! I think I should explain. [*Pause*] I have to confess, Jaques, I wasn't quite happy with things.

Casanova: What things?

Costa: I don't think she was quite convinced and...

Casanova: Convinced? About what? About ME?! Didn't I do it Costa?

Costa: Do you mean I as you or you as you?

Casanova: Me as me! It's important that I did it!

[*Pause*]

Costa: You as you. Yes you did it.

[*CASANOVA sighs gratefully*]

And she enjoyed it! You saw how happy...

Costa: O, but that could have been politeness! A ploy. To make you feel comfortable so that she could then leave.

Casanova: [*Petulantly*] No, no, no! I would know if I'd failed her!

Costa: But you didn't fail her. I did. Only, sadly, me as you! In the preliminary stages....I think we may be about to lose her. I'M THINKING of your reputation!

Casanova: What went wrong?

Costa: I don't know! I had to drug her. But you know that: you shared in the drugs.

Casanova: [*Surprised*] Did I?

Costa: You see? Too much drugs, not enough sex. This is what worries me! That she may have only dreamed the sex under the spell of the drugs.

Casanova: This is outrageous! If you can't be trusted over such a simple matter...

Costa: That's the problem: it's not a simple matter! I'M NOT A SEDUCER! When it comes to the marquises it's an act I've learned to perform well.

Casanova: Good God! This is so depressing! We've come this far...it was hardly seduction! You were doing it for me! It would have been seduction if you'd been doing it for yourself! What are we to do? This is like a conquest without a flag to raise! Someone's bound to notice!

Costa: The meal....

Casanova: [*Dismissively*] Pffft! A meal!

Costa: Yes!

Casanova: I want her hoisted! She'll be my flag!

Costa: I couldn't agree with you more! And the power of the menu will do it!

Casanova: You're talking to the quintessential connoisseur! I have sat at some tables!

Costa: Exactly! Good! Now, as you know, there IS no food in Paris....

Casanova: So?

Costa: I mean that's the general perception...

Casanova: I've told you: we'll go ahead without it.

Costa: It *is* a technical point but...well, anyway, I have a plan!

Casanova: [*Angrily*] Technical! You see? You petit bourgeois! You do not understand what it is to be great! [*Pause*] For example, a great lover as I've tried tirelessly to show, knows that you don't need the intercourse to enjoy the conquest. This is a revolution in sexual thought that I am responsible for! Why can't you respond to its aesthetic charms? It's quite different from all that noisome pumping!

[*Silence*]

Costa: I see all that, of course. Clear as a bell. [*Pause*] What I'm talking about is the female perception...the, if you like, pre-revolutionary position.

Casanova: This is clearly a form of congress that's escaped me! Who's on top?

Costa: [*Sighs*] Angelique believes that there's no food in Paris. Now, I've saved something from the small profits of your reputation - those offerings from our grateful patrons - hoping to use it to escape Paris. I see now that that's a futile hope. Much more important is our happiness here within this small world you've engineered. When I produce the food tomorrow she'll be convinced that it was an act of magic conjured up by you and from that moment will be as devoted to your cause and reputation as...as I have been. And I'm quite sure that given her gregarious nature...

Casanova: What do you mean!

Costa: She plays the violin! Around the whole city! You're reputation can only be enhanced!

[*Silence*]

Casanova: You'll do this for me?

Costa: Yes!

[*Pause*]

Casanova: Give up your nest egg to ensure my immortality?

Costa: I want you to become confident and strong!

[CASANOVA reaches down for COSTA's head which is between his legs and kisses it]

Casanova: I'm still not sure about the food... She needs to be convinced my ME; by my skills, not a cow's tongue or a bayonne ham...

Costa: But Jaques!...

Casanova: Where would you get it?

Costa: I have a friend who has a friend atached to the Committee for Public Safety... Angelique may even reason that she'll never have to worry about food again!

Casanova: I'll defer to your skills of scheming: see if you can't bring a few goose gizzards too. And some scopolo wine!

[COSTA dries CASANOVA]

[CASANOVA lays back down on the bed with a great sigh]

Costa: I'll have to make sure that the food's in place ready for her arrival; or we can have it hidden and all you'll have to do is reveal it!

Casanova: To be honest, I'm surprised there's any money left! I'd thought that carriage, table, theatre and all the other little expenditures necessary to maintain life had brought us to the end of our resources!

[COSTA looks at audience with exasperation]

Casanova: O, and Costa, you'd better put a note on the door saying we're out tomorrow.

[Lights down]

[In the blue light ANGELIQUE comes forward and speaks to audience as CASANOVA dresses]

Angelique: *[To audience]* Costa is a woman! I'm shocked! I'm confused! But why does she persist in the deception with me? Maybe...she thinks that she will have to do it! So that then I can believe that it can be done: that if he can't do it there will be someone who can! But how can SHE do it? Does she realise that we must have an ejaculation? This MUST be achieved! My mistress would know! Age hasn't yet stripped the senses from her womb. There must be a way of doing it...

[She absent-mindedly describes the shape of a penis with her hands]

Angelique: But no! Think! When I first came in here not only did I think that the woman who is Costa is a man but that that man was Casanova! That Casanova was his mother! This is overwhelming! She has the power to ensure that it is done! She must have! What an incomparable power that a woman can make other women believe that she's Casanova! Such a woman can make this Casanova believe in himself again! She can put a magic into him that can make it happen! [*Pause*] The thought of what she does takes my breath away!

[*She goes to where she prepares her entrance*]

[*Blue light down*]

Scene Four

CASANOVA is learning a menu. He is pacing, referring to a piece of paper now and again and speaking some of the words etc.

He is dressed as though he were going out.

There is a knock.

CASANOVA goes.

He returns with ANGELIQUE who is also dressed up. She comes into the room and looks around (for COSTA) without letting CASANOVA be aware of this.

CASANOVA bows, flourishing a silk handkerchief.

Casanova: Angelique! Delighted.

Angelique: [*Fearfully*] Why are you waving that french letter at me?

Casanova: [*Bemused*] What? Good heavens, it's a handkerchief!

[*With great charm, grace and decorum, CASANOVA takes ANGELIQUE's cloak etc. and settles her at the table*]

[*When CASANOVA speaks the menu he does so with relish as though he were eating. Vowels should be large like a mouth being filled, consonants crisp or chewy. There is also a certain feverishness about it all*]

[*CASANOVA sits*]

[*They sit in silence for a moment*]

Angelique: May I have some chocolate?

Casanova: Angelique! What is a cup of chocolate to you at this moment? An impoverishing tickle in the blossoming of your desire; a bad joke at the climax of the pantomime!

Angelique: But I need something.

Casanova: And I have so much to give!

[*He removes the urn*]

[*As he speaks, he lays the table but with empty plates and dishes*]

[*Silence*]

Casanova: Premier service: [*Pause*] Deux oilles: Une au coulis de lantilles, une a la paysanne, Deux potages: un aux laitues, une chiffonâde. Huit hors d'oeuvres; une gallantine d'oseille, d'harricots a la Brétonne, d'harrangs frais a la moutarde, de Maquereaux à la Maitre d'Hotel, une ommelette aux croutons, de morüe à la creme, d'harrangs frai à la mout et de petits pâtés. [*Pause*] You are in the presence of what? Who? Jaques Casanova? Well, I am nothing if not a revolutionary! I embody nothing if not the revolution! So it's no longer enough to say simply: Jaques Casanova. The Terror wants to scare me! But they can't chase off an idea so easily! What is this idea? I am the wind! I sweat stars! I've become what people will say about me from now until the end of time! I am the first example in history of the most basic truth about the world moulded into a philosophy: that nothing's what it seems to be. I'm telling you this for several reasons, one of which is that today I AM GOING TO FEED YOU! We've come to the point where it's almost necessary that we don't shit on the philosophy by making too close a correlation between SOMETHING THAT'S DONE and THE ONE WHO'S SUPPOSED TO HAVE DONE IT! Today, I'm going to surprise you, excite you in a most unimaginable way: bring you, perhaps, to the point of death and as I lay upon your coffin wherein I've driven my nails, you'll sigh with the deepest sigh of gratitude that you came. For you will come. And so, the first great revelation of the day, a day that will change your life is that it wasn't me who disappointed you last night but Costa!

[*Mock surprise from ANGELIQUE*]

Casanova: Deuxieme service: Quatre grandes entrées: un brochet a la pollonnoise, une hure de saumon au four, une carpe au courboüillon, une truite a la chambore. Quatre moyennes: De solles aux fines herbes, de truites grillées sauce hachei, de perches a la Hollandoise, de perches au blanc, de lottes a L'Allemande, de raye au beure noir, de saumon grillé, et de saumon grillé encore. Now, you see, your disappointment is not what it seems. Because now you see that you're disappointed because it wasn't me! And though it may seem to make you a student of philosophy, it does suggest that the best is yet to come! Because you're to be entirely enveloped in the idea of Casanova! Troisieme service! Huit plates de rost. De solles, de filets de brochets fris, de limandes frites, de truites, de carlets au blanc, une queüe de saumon, de solles et quatre salades. I have proved by the exercise of my reputation - which is at its greatest BECAUSE IT'S BEING CREATED AT SUCH

A TIME OF ANTIPATHY TO ITS PURPOSE, that it's what lies behind the general perception that's real, and so, though Costa will describe the activities of my reputation to those who come to experience it - ie, he does the fucking - forgive my bluntness - it's of negligible interest that it's not actually ME doing it because it all serves the idea. Quatrieme service! Huit entremets chauds. De choux fleures Parmezan, un pain aux champignons, de rotties aux anchoyes, un ragout meslé, d'artichaux frits, d'harricots verds, de choux-raves d'epinards. Aussi, quatre assiettes en coquilles, deux assiettes de petits pots, deux assiettes de patisserie. If I may be so bold Angelique, I'd like to tell you that you're about to be fucked by the IDEA of Casanova, just as: finalement: quatre froids. Un buisson d'ecrevisses, un gateau a la bavierre, un poupelaine et un brioche. I have fed you full with words and made the merest potato unnecessary!

[*Pause*]

Angelique: I'm suprised you could remember such a mouthful!

[*Silence*]

Casanova: What?

Angelique: And you've made me hungry. Where's the food?

[*CASANOVA gets up angrily*]

Casanova: What?!

[*Pause*]

Angelique: [*Forcing a laugh*] You haven't fed me! [*Anxiously*] What I mean is... I can't see any food!

Casanova: Food! I suppose last night we didn't make love!

Angelique: You just said we didn't.

Casanova: But we did because it was done! I tell you it's sufficient for me to speak sex to a woman to impregnate her!

[*ANGELIQUE looks anxious*]

Casanova: Reputation! I can do anything without doing it!

Angelique: But you can't eat without eating! You can't do IT without doing it!

Casanova: I can! In fact, I will NOT do it! Just BECAUSE others do it!

Angelique: Not without...without seed.

Casanova: Without seed, foreplay, climax - you name it!

[*ANGELIQUE jumps up*]

Angelique: Climax?! Seed?! We must have seed!

Casanova: What?

Angelique: Why'm I wasting my time here? We must have seed and you can't do it! The seed would prove the magic and the magic would give us food! No, no! I mean the food would have proved the magic which would have given us the seed after the food had proved that climax is given on a plate!

[*They look at each other bewilderedly*]

Angelique: Where's bloody Costa!

Casanova: [*Increasingly angry*] Costa! Costa! What d'you mean?

[*CASANOVA goes to ANGELIQUE and takes her roughly*]

[*He kisses her. She struggles*]

[*They get to the bed. She falls face down on the bed*]

[*CASANOVA falls on top of her. She lets out a groan – she's winded*]

[*CASANOVA gets up clumsily*]

[*He attempts to undo his* culottes *without success*]

Casanova: [*Madly*] The man who remembers his menus is like a great lover. The great lover has to recall and remember his many conquests for the sake of his reputation. In gastronomy, a host who is unknowledgable about the finest meats and cheeses will leave his guests with no experience of love just as he would leave his mistress with a belly-ache. In fact the two things are so closely connected that only a man who remembers what he's eaten can leave his mistress feeling full after sex!

[*He pushes her skirts up and is about to pull down her drawers as COSTA come on*]

[*COSTA speaks while at the door. i.e. doesn't see CASANOVA around the corner*]

Costa: [*Breathless*] There's been a killing.

[*CASANOVA continues to pull at ANGELIQUE's drawers but without success*]

Costa: [*Angry that there's no response*] Very well! I DID say: is your penis still in.

Casanova: [*Outraged*] What! But there's nothing but killing! Even copulation is murdered! Get out!

Costa: [*Still not seeing CASANOVA*] There's been a VERY IMPORTANT killing!

Casanova: Costa! Your persistence shows a shameless indifference to decency! D'you bring the food?

[*COSTA comes around bed and sees CASANOVA*]

Costa: [*Horrified*] What're you doing?

[*CASANOVA lets out a groan of fatigue and gets off ANGELIQUE*]

[*ANGELIQUE groans*]

Casanova: Did you bring the food? I'm starving!

[*Pause*]

Casanova: You didn't! I can see now!

[*CASANOVA goes angrily to COSTA*]

Casanova: [*Threateningly*] What's going on here? She wants your seed! She told me: "I must have seed!" She said she wants YOUR seed! This was after I told her it was you last night not me. So go on, show her! Do her now so that she know's she's done! [*Ironically*] Ha! Give her a handful of your seed. COSTA!

[*COSTA slumps into chair*]

[*Silence*]

[*CASANOVA suddenly runs for his sword which he draws and, returning to COSTA holds at his throat*]

Casanova: Go on! or I'll give you a little prick of my own to help you on your way! Or maybe this killing has killed your appetite! Betrayer! When I eat BEEF, as you know, I eat it raw. My white bread soaks up the red blood. When I drink wine, I drink the heaviest blood-like red. When I eat cheese, I like best the cheese that's in a state of putrefaction. In my life I live one step away from death. One step the wrong way and I'm dead. In the practice of my life I don't fool myself that there's no such thing as death. That's why, when I eat and drink, I eat and drink – as Christ himself advised – the blood and the body. I despise a person who hides from death. In death I see that life is active because life includes death. A life without death would be like a dream without sleep. I enjoy a sleep too. I sleep best on a full stomach. If *your* stomach equivocates and allows itself to be undermined by sensibilities more vague than hunger, then it's because you don't understand that it's in the nature of man that he's able to eat in the very face of death. [*Pause*] Will there be food?

Costa: It was my food man who was killed. Executed by the Committee for Public Safety!

Casanova: Why d'you look at me with such resentment? I'VE never been a committee man! And I warned you about them! You fail to see the irony of the times!

Costa: You may as well kill me because our meal ticket isn't the only thing that's dead. *Nequidquam sapit qui sibi non sapit:* His wisdom's vain who for himself's not wise. Why are you so impatient to finish us off Jaques? Is it because you know the end is coming and you want it over and done with? I told you to wait! Half an hour! Now she knows there's no magic. To be honest I thought there was a little magic left in you. But if there was you've used it to spirit away our freedom! And a fortune!

[*ANGELIQUE gets up*]

Casanova: What're you blathering on about?

Costa: No magic! There's no such fucking thing! There's just the Terror and getting away from it!

[*COSTA gets up to go*]

[*CASANOVA angrily pushes him down*]

Casanova: Speak before I fill the lamentable gap left by the gizzards you never brought with [*Sword at stomach*] YOUR OWN!

[*Silence*]

Costa: [*Angrily*] Angelique's mistress, a Madame d'Urfé, who knows you...

[*COSTA looks to ANGELIQUE*]

Angelique: You knew her at the Ball of The Clipped Yew.

Casanova: That! But only today....

Angelique: She was disguised as the Presidente Portail, you as the king...

Casanova: Disguised! That WAS the Presidente!...

Costa: Apparently she's very ugly! She wore a mask!

Casanova: A mask?... Well of course she wore a mask, we all did! But do you mean...she deceived me? She wore her mask to deceive me?! She was UGLY? How ugly?

Costa: [*Impatiently*] Does it matter?

Casanova: Yes!

Angelique: Very ugly.

Casanova: Christ!

[*Silence*]

[*CASANOVA is appalled*]

Casanova: [*Incredulously*] I was duped in my magnificence? That was one of the great nights of my life! I was master of the Presidente Portail! We did it everywhere! All over the palace. On beds of velvet; under beds; on chairs with her on me, with me taking her from behind while she petted the King's chaise longue. On window sills, in hearths, in doorways, in arbours and hedgerows. And even in a tree in sympathy with the ball's theme! And I believed...she behaved so nobly to remain masked through it all! Especially up the tree! And now you're saying I was duped? By a woman? O, god!

[*He sobs*]

[*Silence*]

Costa: She's now very old and doesn't want to die. She's been told of a way of extending her life. By being reborn. That the only person who could help her in this....

Angelique: Saint Germain told her.

Casanova: Saint Germain?! Saint Germain is a charlatan!

Costa: Apparently so...he told her that the only person who could help her in this was you....

Casanova: Wait a minute, wait a minute, this is all bollocks...what reborn, what are you talking about? Eh?

Costa: The idea was that you could impregnate her; that she would bear a boy child; that she would inhabit the body of the boy child and be born again.

Casanova: It can't be done!

Angelique: What can't be?

Casanova: Rebirth! It can't be done!

Angelique: It may have been sufficient merely to impregnate her!

Casanova: Merely!

Costa: Christ, Jaques! We didn't even need the magic!

Casanova: [*Turning on COSTA*] Why didn't you tell me about this?

Costa: How could I tell you! You've lived so far from Reason or reality!...

[*CASANOVA prods COSTA with sword at throat*]

Casanova: You didn't tell me! I am the vanguard of the great bourgeois revolution and you PATRONISE me like that? You make judgements about me, my life, my future without consulting me! You deny me MY right to make such judgements as though you know better than me what I want!

Costa: Forget it, it's over!

[*CASANOVA suddenly flourishes his sword as though he were preparing to fight*]

Casanova: *Nescit vox missa reventi!*

[*COSTA suddenly lunges forward and puts his throat onto sword blade*]

Costa: Go on! Finish me off! You've more of less done that anyway!

Angelique: No!

[*Silence*]

Casanova: What?

Angelique: [*To COSTA*] You knew HE couldn't do it!

Casanova: It CANNOT BE DONE!

Angelique: Costa was protecting you!

Casanova: What?

Angelique: You knew he COULDN'T do it! That's why you didn't tell him. You didn't tell him because you didn't want it to come out that he CANNOT ACTUALLY DO IT! [*Pause*] He's impotent! Isn't that the truth!

[*CASANOVA looks shocked and hurt*]

Casanova: [*To audience*] This is some petit bourgeois trick! It can't be done anyway but they deflect attention from that truth by saying that I can't do it! [*To ANGELIQUE*] You're forgetting: I did it!

Angelique: What? When?

Casanova: Yesterday sweet! WE did it!

Angelique: We didn't! You know we didn't. You TOLD me we didn't!

Casanova: I was lying.

Angelique: You weren't.

Casanova: Would you deny the bourgeois his lies! What is this, anarchy?

Angelique: You didn't do it!

Casanova: Costa, is this true!

[*Silence*]

Costa: I've lived this dilemma: to be myself would mean that he could not be Casanova and so to preserve him I've become an apparent Casanova. I've tried to make him happy and I think that's a moral thing to do. I've lived with so many lies for that nobler intention: "do her and do her good for the reputation!" O, this wise man whose sex has been sublimated to wisdom! Who wisely choses the best MAN for the job of preserving his reputation. His sex hasn't been sublimated: it's gone! Casanova is sexless. He can't do it anymore! This is the truth!

[*Silence*]

[*CASANOVA slumps into chair wretchedly*]

Costa: [*Tearfully*] "Give it to her Costa so that she believes I did it! I conquered her!" That's all it ever means. All it's ever meant! It doesn't matter whose dick is used as long as it's done and seen as his conquest! But the fact is, this is not a branch of scholarship: it's not as if I'm NOT doing it; not as if I were just his surrogate like a student may be to some great philosophy. I DO it! And I've learned to do it in order to go on doing it! And I do it well for whatever purpose I have because [*To CASANOVA*] happiness is extended in humanity by people making each other happy: pure and simple. Not by experiencing happiness for them. Like me making you happy by doing it! But even that doesn't explain why I do what I do: I do it in order that you can survive that storm of murder out there: this great horror in your life; more appalling than your impotence!

Casanova: Horror? Impotence?

Costa: The Terror!

Casanova: I'm not afraid of the Terror!

Costa: The Terror's the revolution! It's new, you're old! It's a metaphor for what happens to us all: death at the hand of youth. *Nequidquam sapit qui sibi non sapit!* You and your fucking memoirs!

[*COSTA picks up manuscript and throws it on the floor*]

[*CASANOVA cries out*]

Casanova: That's my!...

Costa: Vanity! You can't make something new out of what's irreversibly old! We live in the acting out of our lives. Not by erecting tombstones.

[*CASANOVA collects together his papers*]

Costa: The wise application of wisdom! Huh! Food, drink, women!...these are the pursuits of the hedonist! Futile pursuits! Happiness is the pursuit of wisdom not the exploitation of wisdom! Anyway, your wine is coloured water; your food is just words and your women...I do them! [*To ANGELIQUE*] Like I would have done yours!

Angelique: You still can!

Costa: What!

[*Silence*]

[*ANGELIQUE goes to COSTA and pulls at his top revealing a breast tied down with straps*]

[*COSTA turns to hide from her*]

Angelique: I know you're a woman. But it doesn't matter. We've now got the truth. All that matters; all that ever mattered was that she is given seed.

[*CASANOVA suddenly gets up and throws his sword out of the window*]

[*He goes to the dressing table, takes the covering from the mirror and kisses it thus kissing himself*]

[*Between now and the end of the scene he makes up very heavily to hide his face, occasionally passionately kissing the mirror*]

[*SOPHIE slumps into chair*]

Sophie: It can't be done! Now you know!

Angelique: You can do it!

Sophie: There isn't any magic! I was just deceiving you. It's become my life. Being what I'm not. Just to survive. I didn't know it myself until now but I was going to cheat you. [*Pause*] For the last time; IT CANNOT BE DONE! I can't even do the smallest trick of the hand. Our life is ruined. Like his face.

Angelique: But I knew *it* couldn't be done. The whole thing. She knows it too. For one thing, she's too old to have babies! But we don't have to face those things. She'd give her fortune just to relive a night of her youth. And why not? Why shouldn't it cost her that? After all, it was the night when the great Casanova took her. He was everything. He was the old regime. And he made her happy for a night. She simply has to feel his SEED; pathetic though that may be!

[*Silence*]

Angelique: What we need is...we need to make a...

[*ANGELIQUE describes the shape of a penis with her hands*]

Sophie: Prick?

Angelique: Exactly!

[*ANGELIQUE paces as she thinks. She has become master of the situation*]

Angelique: Costa?

Sophie: Sophie.

Angelique: Sophie! Ah! We need a piece of something solid – about eight inches long – but with some flexibility in it. It needs to be able to bend a little. And all the way down the middle of it we need a tubeway, an artery but nothing too big; in fact something very fine. How can we make that?

Sophie: I don't know, Angelique! I don't! I told you, there's no more magic!

Angelique: [*Holding Sophie*] Not magic! Confidence! Build a prick with confidence!

[*Silence*]

Sophie: And this artery would carry what...not sperm?

Angelique: A fluidy substance. And what we need is a kind of small sack or pouch containing two fig-like things and the substance – which may as well be white but must be slightly heavy; heavier than water with a weight to it that needs to be kind of...

Sophie: Gluey?

Angelique: Gooey? Yes. Uchy!

Sophie: No, gluey...well gooey, ok...

Angelique: Something not free-flowing...

Sophie: Persistant....

Angelique: Yes! Unyielding.

Sophie: Obstinate!

Angelique: O, yes, yes! Pig-headed!

Sophie: Bloody-minded!

Angelique: Yes, ha, ha! Self-opinionated and bigoted!

Sophie: A bigoted fluid! Ha, ha!

[*SOPHIE begins to laugh uncontrollably*]

Angelique: Persecuting!

Sophie: What?!

Angelique: Well a bigot persecutes!

Sophie: Ha, ha!

Angelique: Anyway we need to make this sack-thing which we can put on the end of the thing that looks like a penis...

Sophie: A dildo?

Angelique: Exactly!

Sophie: Ha, ha!

Angelique: And if you squeeze it VERY VERY hard, out will come the white bigoted fluid! Can you do it?

[*SOPHIE controls her laughing*]

Angelique: You MUST!

[*Pause*]

Sophie: Yes! Yes! We will go to Dux!

Angelique: [*Pitifully*] Dogs! I haven't gone to the dogs!

Sophie: [*To herself*] It's a place in Bohemia!

[*Lights down*]

[*In the blue light the following takes place*]

Casanova: [*Brokenly*] There's no future Sophie! I'm finished!

Sophie: No future because you're finished?

Casanova: Yes. That's what I said.

Sophie: But that means there's only no future for you.

Casanova: But for me there ISN'T any future without me!

Sophie: Jaques! The whole point about immortality is that it's the future with US. You couldn't be immortal if you weren't gone before your future!

[*CASANOVA's face looks out of the blue horror-struck*]

[*As they prepare for next scene, ANGELIQUE comes forward to audience*]

[*She drags a bath on*]

Angelique: [*To audience*] Everything was arranged. It was agreed that as part of the ritual my mistress would wear a sack over her head. We told her that the magic of the moment would be severely compromised by her ugliness. There was a full moon. I met Sophie to give her the letter for Count Waldstein. That would instruct him to give them my mistress's money.

[*SOPHIE comes on wearing a smock*]

[*She is carrying the (modified) dildo and some paper*]

[*ANGELIQUE and SOPHIE come close to each other*]

[*ANGELIQUE hands SOPHIE the letter*]

[*SOPHIE reads the letter. There are two pages*]

[*They come close to one another as if about to kiss but they don't*]

Angelique: [*To audience*] Everything went well until...until...well, the most extraordinary thing happened. It was extraordinary because in some ways it was so petty. We'll show you. I'll play my mistress.

Scene Five

In the blue light.

[*ANGELIQUE puts a sack over her head*]

[*ANGELIQUE and SOPHIE get into the bath*]

[*SOPHIE places dildo beside bath*]

Angelique: Chevalier.

Sophie: O, please. Call me Jaques, Madame.

Angelique: And you must call me Violette.

Sophie: Violette.

Angelique: I have waited so long Jaques, I had not expected you to be so youthful.

[*ANGELIQUE strokes SOPHIE's arm*]

[*SOPHIE stops her severely*]

Sophie: Proof, surely, that the magic isn't mere sorcery.

[*Silence*]

Angelique: Such a pity I can't see that famous head because of the sack on mine. [*Pause*] Tell me Jaques. PROMISE me. When this is over you will allow me to have your portrait painted so that I may keep it with me ...

Sophie: [*Mock anger*] Violette! I am violently opposed to portraiture. It's the handmaiden of vanity! And vanity is best described by its adjective - vain. All the portraiture in the world will not make a man more known that he deserves!

[*Silence*]

Angelique: Do you hear anything?

Sophie: What?

Angelique: I thought you were listening for something. For, perhaps, some word from the moon. Saint Germain said ...

Sophie: Madame! Saint Germain is a cheap fornicator! And he is dead!

Angelique: I'm sorry Jaques! But why are we waiting?

Sophie: Because I am concentrating! The moon is a mute. It has to speak in its own way. We will call for it to speak.

Angelique: How?

Sophie: Lay back.

[*ANGELIQUE gasps*]

Angelique: This is it!

[*Silence*]

[*SOPHIE picks up the paper she's brought and flourishes it*]

[*ANGELIQUE gasps*]

Angelique: What is it?

Sophie: A letter. A letter to the moon.

Angelique: How will you send it?

Sophie: Fire.

[*SOPHIE 'magically' lights the paper*]

[*SOPHIE chants severely so that ANGELIQUE is afraid*]

Sophie: You have asked the moon: O, lunar mia lunacy, take the scab of womanhood from my eternity - shaman escalavar shur - show me in this lunarium the boy I will be - seethur scee - and how to be him!

[*Ashes fall into bath*]

[*SOPHIE gasps*]

Angelique: [*Fearfully*] What is it?

Sophie: The words. Can you see?

Angelique: No!

Sophie: O, gracious moon! [*To ANGELIQUE*] If you had been able to see them it may have meant that they were only illusory. The fact that only I can see them proves that they're there.

Angelique: But I can't see them because I've got this sack on my head!

Sophie: Violette! Don't raise this question mark against the ritual!

Angelique: [*Contrite*] What do the words say?

[*Silence*]

Sophie: Shit!

Angelique: What is it?

Sophie: The words say that impregnation should take place on the first new moon of the year. O, unhappy hour!

Angelique: What?! What is it!

Sophie: That was last Friday!

[*ANGELIQUE cries out*]

Angelique: Then I'm done for!

Sophie: You could wait until next year.

Angelique: No!

Sophie: Then there's only one thing for it: you must look for a passage to heaven. Utilise sleep.

Angelique: Sleep?

Sophie: Sleep.

Angelique: I'll try.

Sophie: You must believe you are asleep even if you're not. That way it will be as if you are.

[*Silence*]

[*SOPHIE picks up the dildo and puts it in bath*]

[*She moves as though she were preparing to use it when CASANOVA rushes on. He is mad*]

Casanova: Aha!

[*SOPHIE and ANGELIQUE freeze*]

Casanova: Who is this so rarely postured? Offering her fanny to the clittering moon. Why isn't it...it is! The Presidente Portail! O sweet, sweet! I am loathe to disabuse you my beautiful tree-headed wight, but it is not I, your valiant chevalier, your one and only Jaques Casanova at this moment re-rooting you. I have to tell you sweet that in fact you're being shagged by a twelve inch Indian teak dildo!

[*ANGELIQUE cries out*]

[*CASANOVA laughs*]

[*SOPHIE gets up*]

[*She gets out of the bath*]

[*She picks up the letter ANGELIQUE gave her*]

[*ANGELIQUE cries out and then weeps*]

[*SOPHIE goes off*]

Casanova: Sophie! Where you going?

Sophie: [*As she goes*] Dux! Without you!

Casanova: No, no! Take me with you! Don't leave me Sophie! Please!

[*Lights on*]

[*In the blue light they change for the next scene and the end of Saint Saens Requiem can be heard. (This is deliberately anachronistic)*]

Scene Six

CASANOVA is sitting in an armchair in a library (Dux). He is dressed like a woman in late middle-age: floral dress cardigan etc.

He has his feet in a bowl of water.

He is sobbing.

There are books everywhere.

(There must be obviously painted scenery).

On the walls where there aren't books there are photos of nude women as in Pirelli calendars etc. (photos that are made pornographic by failing to explain the innuendos they convey).

SOPHIE is working on clothes; ironing, folding etc. She is wearing a man's dressing gown and slippers and her hair is tied up to make it look short like a man's.

Whenever SOPHIE speaks she has to almost shout to speak directly into CASANOVA's ear.

Casanova: Do you hear that music?

[*Silence*]

Casanova: My mind must be making it up.

[*Silence*]

Casanova: Do you know what that means?

[*Silence*]

Casanova: It means I'm suffering on behalf of others. It's in *my* head.

[*Silence*]

Casanova: I've taken on myself this pain and unhappiness! I'm experiencing the pain and unhappiness of the world as if by proxy!

[*Silence*]

Casanova: *Ecce homo!*

Sophie: [*Reflectively*] *Ecce homo?* [*Pause*] What does it mean?

Casanova: It was said of Christ. Behold the man! His greatness was not that he paid for man's crimes but that he had to suffer as a man for being a god! It's the same with me!

Sophie: But Jack! Christ was innocent.

[*SOPHIE wipes CASANOVA's feet*]

Casanova: [*Angrily*] If he was innocent then he wasn't real. Evil is innocent!

[*Silence*]

Casanova: I am real. [*Motions towards memoirs*]

[*She gets him to the bed. She undresses him down to his underclothes*]

Casanova: [*Getting into bed*] The people have a predisposition for creating life out of deception. My memoirs will do them a favour! [*Pause*] I've revalued value! I've made Art of deception and virtue of vice and cheating. I've written the bourgeois blueprint. A bible of lies that Europe will turn into a philosophy for its politics! [*Feverishly*] I've got a new beginning! For the book: Man is born moral yet everywhere he sins. [*Pause*] No! SOME men are born moral and yet everywhere THEY sin. [*Pause*] No, no! What was it?! If *some* men are born moral then ALL men are born moral. You cannot have a moral law for one that's meaningful if it's not a moral law for all. [*Pause*] Man is NOT born free that is why everywhere he sins. [*Pause. "Happily"*] Perhaps some men ARE born free and hence they cannot sin!

[*Silence*]

[*SOPHIE puts a blanket over him*]

Sophie: Is that it?

Casanova: Yes!

Sophie: It's rubbish.

Casanova: What...? Sophie! Don't speak like that, it frightens me!

Sophie: What?

Casanova: It makes me feel lonely!

Sophie: But Jack. The only reason I'm here is to protect you from loneliness. [*Pause*] We'll use the beginning we've got. The people don't want philosophy. If they did they'd want your Rousseaus and your Robespierres. And they don't. You're right: they don't want truth. Entertainment! That's what you've given them all your life. That's what you'll give them from beyond the grave.

Casanova: [*Appalled*] That's what it's come to? I'm a clown? But I'm wise! I've all along, all my life been wise! *Nequidquam sapit qui sibi non sapit!* [*Tearful*] Sophie, I feel so depressed! What is life? Nothing more than a god masturbating. [*Pause*] ...Did I ever tell you about Leah?

[*Silence*]

Casanova: [*Often feverishly*] I met her, I remember, in a town near Venice. She was a young Jewish girl. A virgin. Her father had invited me to stay with his family. She was so pure. And unapproachable and engaged to be married to a Jewish boy she'd never seen. For these reasons I had to have her.

[*SOPHIE wipes CASANOVA's brow*]

Casanova: She used to come to my room at breakfast-time bringing me goose livers to eat. Then I invited her to my room for dinner. We ate liver again and drank Scopolo wine. Leah wore a beautiful fichu over her beautiful tits. She said she loved me but wouldn't kiss me even though, she said, I had a handsome mouth. I have to make this girl an animal so that I can take her! It's what she wants, I know, but her religion and her morality forbids her. One day I bought some shell fish which it's against her religion to eat. If I can get her to eat some of the shell fish then I've established that she'll break the laws of her religion. When the maid's left I offer some to Leah. She eats. So! She's not so pure! The next morning at breakfast, Leah brings my chocolate and I think to myself: I'll show her my miniatures and engravings. I showed her first the picture of a woman lying on her back, stark naked and masturbating. I could see Leah's pulse quicken. She said that she did that too! That made my prick hard. I next showed her the collection of illustrations for Aretino which show different positions for fucking. She admires them calmly and says that a decent girl shouldn't look too long at these things because they can arouse strong emotions. I told her I agree and showed her my erection. I calmed myself like a schoolboy.

One night, unable to sleep, I walked downstairs and saw a room with a light on. I looked in and saw Leah stark naked on the bed practising postures with a young man in the same state. They were no more than two paces from the door and I saw everything perfectly. After a while the young man assumed the straight tree position and while he ate her cunt she drank his sperm.

[*CASANOVA is excited by now and it's causing him some pain*]

Sophie: Jack, leave it! You're hurting yourself!

Casanova: [*Feverishly even angrily*] The next day I told her what I'd seen and told her I hoped she'd do as much for me the next night if only to keep her secret safe. I might otherwise feel it my moral duty to tell her father Mordecai what I'd seen. She said in anger that she didn't love me. She left. [*Pause*] But she returned. [*Pause*] I knew girls of Leah's kind. They're not uncommon. I'd known her like in Spa, Geneva, London and even Venice!

It was Saturday. That night Leah came to see me. She said she wanted to speak. To justify herself. Justice was with me! I'd been seriously offended by her! She said she loved me. She said she was young and had uncontrollable desires. She said she had the misfortune to be in love with the young Christian I'd seen her with, who was a beggar and a libertine; who didn't love her and who she paid! YOUNG! Doesn't she think that I have been young? I invented it! All youth cultures come from me! She said I was the cause of her having drunk the Christian's sperm that night because I'd aroused her with my engravings and my wine!

[*CASANOVA is seized suddenly and momentarily with a spasm*]

Sophie: Jack!

Casanova: I was only waiting for her to break then I'd humiliate her. But she was artful! I keep seeing her with the Christian's prick in her mouth. His balls like fresh figs hanging about the opened fig of her mouth.

[*He cries out in pain*]

Casanova: Look Sophie! Feel!

[*He takes SOPHIE's hand and puts it beneath the blanket*]

[*He takes his hand away leaving her's there*]

Casanova: She knew I had this image and she tormented me with it. For days she played this game then on the fifteenth night Leah came to my room. She abandoned her petticoat and shift and lay down beside me.

[*SOPHIE takes her hand away*]

[*She substitutes his hand for hers*]

[*CASANOVA masturbates as he speaks*]

[*Pause*]

Casanova: [*With difficulty*] Saying nothing she clasped me to her breast. She sat astride me and deluged me with kisses. In no time my caresses were like hers. And still I was silent! I devoured her tits and then I spoke. [*Pause*] I said "You can't bury me except by unlocking that very tomb!" She assented. [*Seized*] I fucked her without delay for I had delayed enough! [*Pause*] And I fucked her and fucked her and fucked her!

[*He has an orgasm*]

Casanova: *Cursum perficio!*

[*He cries out terribly and then falls silent*]

[*SOPHIE leans over CASANOVA*]

[*She gently closes his eyes as though she were putting him to sleep*]

Sophie: We'll use it. We'll tone down the language. People won't read it if it's ill-mannered. If you're owed ANYTHING by your bourgeois revolution it's the right to be bourgeois. Even to dupe the future if it wants to be duped by you.

[*She pauses*]

[*She sniffs back a tear*]

[*She begins packing her things as she speaks*]

[*She takes off the dressing gown and dresses in woman's clothes*]

Sophie: [*To audience*] So in the end he came and died. [*Pause*] Why did I stay with him? As a dutiful wife would? No. Perhaps as a friend. [*Pause*] By the time we had arrived in Dux Madame D'Urfé had already sent a letter to Count Waldstein telling him that under no circumstances was he to give any of the money to anyone until Casanova had died. So Jack was obliged to take a job as librarian [*She indicates library*] and I was obliged to wait for his death to get the money! In the memoirs I've suggested that he was here for twelve years. I think that's sadder. In fact, it was barely twelve months. Then Angelique wrote. To inform me of the death of her mistress. Madame d'Urfé didn't last long after what happened. What a sad dramatic irony: that the exercise that was meant to let her live forever, killed her within a week. [*Pause*] But you don't know everything. You're restless. You want to know where I'm going now. I'm going to her. [*Pause*] It's still not enough is it? You want more?

[*She takes out letter*]

Sophie: It's the letter she gave me the night we attended to Madame d'Urfé. When she gave me the letter to Count Waldstein.

[*She opens the letter and reads*]

Sophie: "Dear Sophie,

I have discovered that I love you.

When we first kissed I felt mysteriously drawn to you. I say 'mysteriously' because I thought you were a man and there is nothing about men that I've found attractive. The mystery was solved quite quickly when I confronted what I knew deep-down: that you were a woman. But what I did was, I said to myself: this gives her an extraordinary power! This woman who dresses as a man and does all those things with those women - the duchesses etcetera. She can put magic into HIM. I fooled myself into believing this! Why? Because I didn't want to lose you. Which meant that I loved you. And you continued your pretence not because you thought it would help you in the project but because you were falling in love with me!

I can confess: I'm no longer interested in what happens to my mistress; she's had a long life. And I'm afraid I've used this whole episode with her as a substitute pursuit for what I should really be doing with my own. Now I've come to face what that is, things are so much clearer! For example, Casanova, this man of ALL men turned you away from men! I'm sure of this. Though I don't think you knew this until you met me. But isn't that the ultimate irony? Not quite! There's a bigger one.

Everything about your life and your power over sex drew me ineluctably into your world. Sucked me in. You have a power in these things that no man - not even Casanova - could ever have! But what predisposed me to be so drawn to you? My mistress! You see, what Casanova was never able to create was a world of sex to which you - or anyone - would want to belong. Instead, he created a world in which the purity of sexual desire is destroyed. My mistress was ruined that night that she posed as the Presidente Portail; the night she was so overwhelmed by him. It turned her into a woman who would do ANYTHING to achieve a lascivious end. Which is a process that can never be satisfied. Imagine a people who spend their whole lives pursuing one greater sensation after another. Finally they must turn to killing. I know about these things because in her pursuit for the ultimate sensation - which I believe she felt would come to her the night of her rebirth - she corrupted me." [*Pause*] "BUT...the wheel has come full circle because the power unleashed the night Casanova corrupted my mistress can now be reborn - revolutionised, for our perfect happiness.

Come to me as soon as you can and I will show you!"

[*SOPHIE picks up dildo and puts it in case*]

[*She pauses*]

[*She takes the dildo out again*]

Sophie: I won't need this. [*To CASANOVA*] I don't need to pretend that I'm a man anymore.

[*She takes dildo and places it in the dead hand of CASANOVA*]

Sophie: Behold the woman!

[*Lights down*]

END

Looking for the World

For Edward Bond

Looking for the World was first performed on 13th May 1986 at the Sherman Theatre, Cardiff, by the Sherman Theatre Company and Made in Wales. The play was directed by Roland Rees and designed by Berard Culshaw, with the following cast:

PADDY MILLANE ....Howell Evans

SYLVIA MILLANE ....Patricia Kane

YANNIS PETROU ....William Maxwell

MELINE PETROU..Mary Ellen Ray

MICHALIS PETROU...Andrew Phylactou

NANA LEROS...Malya Woolf

CHARACTERS:

PADDY MILLANE	- British man about 55
SYLVIA MILLANE	- His wife, British, about 55
YANNIS PETROU	- Dark-skinned Greek man about 45
MELINA PETROU	- His wife, dark-skinned, Greek, about 45
MICHALIS PETROU	- Their son, dark-skinned, 20
NANA LEROS	- A woman who looks like a beggar

PLACE: A Greek island in the Aegean. The action is set in the square outside the central hotel in the main town (which is, in fact, little more than a village).

TIME: Sometime in the late 1960's during the period in which the Colonel's Junta ruled Greece.

ACCENTS

The Greeks should speak without any accent. This is important. The only possible alternative is that they speak with accents that are unBritish. Most probably American, but then they must all speak with the same accent.

The Milannes speak with a British accent, ideally a Cardiff one.

When the Greeks speak in English they speak with a Greek accent.

Part One

Scene One

Scene: *Evening*

At the back of the stage to the right, diagonally, there are steps like those that may be found in front of a Greek Temple. They are the steps leading into the hotel of YANNIS and MELINA PETROU. The steps were white but are now dirty and worn and signify dilapidation. Nothing is seen of the front of the hotel.

In the space to the left centre of these steps - which is the square - there are three or four tables each with two or three chairs at it. Table and chairs look grubby.

There is a line stretching from somewhere behind the steps to somewhere centre-back of stage. From this line there is a small octopus hanging, drying.

Near the far left hand table there is a bird table and a bird bath.

NANA LEROS, who looks like a beggar, comes on. She goes to the birdbath and table and investigates them.

Nana: No water. No food. The birds ought to be glad when Michalis returns. [*Short pause*] But who knows? [*She goes to step*] Melina! [*Silence. She sits*] Melina is the mother. This is the Central Hotel. The family home of the Petrous. Michalis, their son, is coming home tomorrow. [*Pause*] Michalis is like his mother. [*Pause*] Michalis WAS like his mother. [*Pause*] Michalis was like his mother WAS.

[*Silence*]

His mother was always kind but strong. This strength you show off to the world. She was wise. She spoke with the voice of quiet reason. [*Pause*] Of course, there are some things...[*Short pause*] What does a family exist for? For security. The reasoning goes: if a brutal father were denounced before the world, the unity of the family would be threatened. Why have family or father, if either one can threaten the other? So the brutality is hidden and the security of the family is undisturbed.

[*Silence*]

Melina!

[*Silence*]

Here is what I think: if they let me sleep in there tonight, it's a good omen. Melina!

[*MELINA comes to top of steps*]

Melina: What do you want Nana?

Nana: The nights get cold Melina. Especially when you're alone. Without communion.

Melina: This is not a church.

Nana: I don't need a church. In church you hide away from the influence of evil, you don't fight it. A true communion does.

Melina: I don't know what you mean Nana. What evil?

[*MELINA yawns*]

Nana: How would you best like to welcome Michalis? With birds dancing on his table? [*Indicates birdtable*] Or with more sadness?

Melina: [*Sighing*] Come in.

[*NANA goes up steps*]

[*Lights down*]

Scene Two

Scene: *Night*

A bright light floods out over the steps, coming from the inside of the hotel.

Bouzouki music is being played quite loud in the hotel. The piece is "Ti St' Anathema In 'Afto" by Manos Tacticos.

MELINA comes quickly out of the hotel, down the steps. She is controlling an anger. She pauses.

PETROU comes out after her.

Petrou: Things have changed, Melina, and you chose to let them change.

Melina: I didn't choose to...

Petrou: Then who did? Colonel Papadopoulos? You didn't object. Your silence...

[*She is about to say something and he motions her not to with a threatening glance*]

Petrou: ...meant you chose.

Melina: Yannis, she wants a bed for the night. The first time since Michalis has been away. She wants to welcome him home!

Petrou: Michalis is now an officer in the army...

Melina: He's only been away three months.

Petrou: You accept that or you don't. You can't have it both ways...

Melina: What are you talking about? Our life has never been like that. I don't want to live in a way that I have to choose between ...ouzo and water. I like to mix a bit of both. Michalis has always cared for Nana. Are you saying that because he's an officer in the army...

Petrou: What kind of thing is that? A bird that can't fly that a boy might lose his head over for a few days. Only with him it goes on as if it was some escape...some acropolis in the clouds. And because his mother...

Melina: [*Angrily*] Because his father...

Petrou: [*Bullying*] Because his mother has encouraged him into a woman's ways TO MAKE HIM HERS.

Melina: That's not true Yannis. Michalis is naturally a kind boy...

Petrou: [*Ignoring her*] But let me tell you this: he will be coming home in uniform..."naturally a kind boy". Do you mean the crying? He will be coming home in uniform and his new life is what will be encouraged. [*Indicating inside hotel*] This will never happen again. Who wants a family, that kind of GOD-BLESSED thing and at the same time a hotel in the heart of the family for diseased beggars?

Melina: And what if Michalis rejects his uniform because you're changing his life for him? Who will even HAVE a family then?

Petrou: There won't be one as long as she stays. Because if she stays, I go.

[*Silence*]

Petrou: You understand this, Melina: the past is dead.

[*MELINA begins to go off*]

Melina: I'm surprised you haven't painted the table and chairs.

Petrou: Why paint them? We've got an empty hotel. Anyway, who wants to drink with a tramp?

[*MELINA pauses*]

Melina: We've got an empty hotel, Yannis, because there are no tourists. And there are no tourists because people think they're going to get assassinated in the streets by our army.

[*MELINA goes off*]

Petrou: [*Shouting after her*] If that's what our army wanted, they'd go into THEIR streets and do it!

[*He pauses. He makes a sound of disgust. He goes back into the hotel*]

[*After a moment, a cry comes from inside the hotel. A moment later, NANA comes out clutching her side, slightly bent over, she goes quickly down the steps*]

[*PETROU comes out to the top of the steps*]

Petrou: [*Shouting after her*] Don't fucking come back, Nana Leros! This is a decent hotel! [*He laughs*]

[*NANA rushes off across the square*]

[*PETROU looks around him and breathes deeply. He goes into the hotel*]

[*The music is changed to "Nostalgia" by Manos Tacticos*]

[*PETROU comes back out. He carries a drink. He stops on the steps and looks about him admiringly. He goes down steps and puts drink on table. He begins to dance to the music*]

Petrou: [*As he dances*] Yes Michalis. You're not the only one who was a young man in Athens. IN A UNIFORM. Girls! I remember. [*Pause*] Summer along the city street. Summer of your life. Nights around the city. Life on the loose. ON THE LOOSE. A warrior's life. Away from the home. The family. Putting on a uniform and the life of the warrior. Parade proudly before the girls and YOU ARE GREEK. [*Pause*] I remember.

[*The siren sounds*]

[*PETROU rushes into the hotel*]

[*Most of the light goes. The remaining light is tinged with reds and greens*]

[*MELINA comes on hurriedly. She goes into the hotel*]

[*The music stops*]

[*There is a distant scream*]

[*PETROU comes out*]

Melina: [*From inside hotel*] Yannis, what was that?

Petrou: Someone breaking the curfew.

Melina: [*Worriedly*] Why do people do it?

Petrou: Exactly, Melina. And if we didn't have the curfew, we wouldn't know that there were people around ready to break it.

Melina: [*Urgently*] Come in.

[*PETROU goes down steps. He begins to put chairs against tables*]

Melina: Come in Yannis!

Petrou: We're allowed to put our house in order, Melina. We're not anti-government.

[*He picks up drink and finishes it*]

Melina: [*At top of steps*] But Yannis. I thought you respected the change.

[*Lights down*]

Scene Three

Scene: *Early morning*

A bright, white light everywhere.

NANA can just be seen lurking, keeping an eye on PETROU and MELINA who don't see her.

MELINA comes on. She carries a bowl of olives which she puts on the table. She takes the octopus from the line.

Nana: Is that octopus for Michalis or could it BE Michalis?

[*MELINA looks around her but can't see NANA*]

Melina: Nana?

Nana: All stretched out with no soul left.

Melina: Go away Nana!

[*PETROU comes on. He carries a banner with the words: "Welcome home Officer Petrou." He hangs it on the line where the octopus was*]

[*PETROU is now wearing the shirt and trousers of a policeman's uniform. He pauses*]

Petrou: An officer! In the army!

[*MELINA looks concerned*]

[*PETROU goes back in. His step has become militaristic though in a calm, measured way. He pauses and turns to MELINA*]

Petrou: Melina, are you going to leave those olives there?

Melina: Yes.

Petrou: They could get stolen.

Melina: [*Bemused*] By who?

Petrou: By Nana.

[*Silence*]

Melina: There was a time when olives were as free as the air.

Petrou: Beggars like Nana think everything's free.

Melina: No Yannis. If she thought everything was free, she'd live like a very rich lady.

[*Pause*]

Petrou: Cover them or they'll dry before he's home.

[*PETROU goes off up steps*]

[*MELINA begins to go off after him*]

Nana: Melina! Are you going to feed the birds?

Melina: Go away Nana! Michalis is coming home today and I don't want any trouble.

Nana: Do you want him to come home to a home or a billet?

[*Silence*]

Nana: [*Coming to where she can be seen by MELINA*] You know, it's possible that to protect your family you'll stop seeing what's happening in the world.

Melina: My family IS my world.

Nana: There's a world outside. And it's threatening.

Melina: The only threat to me and my family, Nana, that could mean anything, would have to come from inside it. And...

Nana: But if you can see that!... or perhaps the wife has slept too long in her husband's bed.

Melina: [*Threateningly*] Nana!

Nana: You must fight for Michalis. Begin now! [*Pointing to bird table*] Put food on the table.

Melina: For the last time, go away!

[*MELINA goes off up steps*]

[*NANA circles the table once. She pauses at the table with the olives. She stands up defiantly and goes off but can still be seen*]

[*PETROU comes on with a Greek flag. He hangs it next to the banner*]

[*MELINA comes on. She carries a tray with water and glasses. On the tray are some crumbs of food to put on the bird table. She puts the tray on a table*]

[*MELINA puts some water into the bird bath*]

[*PETROU leaves the flag*]

Petrou: [*To MELINA*] What are you doing?

Melina: I'm putting water in the birdbath.

Petrou: [*Irritably*] Why? Why today?

[*Pause*]

[*PETROU goes to MELINA and knocks the birdbath down*]

Melina: [*Controlling her anger*] Yannis, there will be a day...

Petrou: But NOT today.

[PETROU returns to flag]

[MELINA goes to table. She picks up some crumbs from the tray and takes them to the birdtable]

[PETROU turns to her. He lets the flag drop and rushes to MELINA angrily]

Petrou: I said NOT TODAY!

[MELINA stands between PETROU and the bird-table]

Melina: Then let him decide!

[PETROU pauses. He looks bemused]

Melina: I could say, too, Yannis, that finally, today, you will not...NOT today again. But I want Michalis to be happy to be home. So I say, let's leave it up to Michalis. Let Michalis decide about today.

[NANA looks apprehensive]

[PETROU looks pensive. He goes back to flag with a kind of confidence]

[MELINA picks up the birdbath. She puts it on the birdtable. She pauses. She turns to listen]

Melina: Yannis, can you hear something!

[PETROU turns from flag and listens towards sea, off right]

Petrou: Only the sound of the sea.

Melina: No Yannis! That's the sound of a boat! In the mist. It's Michalis!

[NANA looks half glad and half anxious]

[MELINA and PETROU come together and look off. They don't touch]

[Sound of ship's hooter]

[Lights down]

Scene Four

Scene: *A short time later.*

PETROU can be seen peeping out to look for MICHALIS.

MICHALIS PETROU walks on. He seems older than his twenty years. He wears an immaculate uniform with a peaked cap. He wears the cap pulled over his eyes as if to hide them. He carries a kit bag over his shoulder. He is morose.

He stands centrally for a moment looking up above the steps. He drops the kit bag.

PETROU comes out of the hotel quickly to welcome MICHALIS. He carries a tray with a jug of rezina and glasses.

There is a cloth on the olives. MELINA follows PETROU a little less certainly.

Petrou: Welcome home Michalis!

Melina: [*A little after PETROU, but almost together with him*] Welcome home Michalis.

[*They come down the steps to meet him*]

[*NANA comes on to watch but can't be seen by the others*]

[*MELINA anxiously hugs MICHALIS who is a little cold*]

[*PETROU puts the tray on the table. He takes the cloth off the olives with a little flourish*]

Petrou: Let's drink!

Melina: Sit down Michalis. You must be tired. You look it.

[*MICHALIS remains standing and MELINA's anxiety remains*]

Michalis: [*Worriedly*] Do you have any visitors?

Melina: What sort of visitors?

Michalis: [*Uncertainly*] Tourists.

Petrou: The world has designated Greece a lepers' colony. You should know that Michalis. We haven't had tourists for months.

Michalis: That makes things easier.

Melina: Yes.

Petrou: We won't be disturbed. You can tell us your stories through the night.

Michalis: I don't have much to say. [*Pause*] I have a lot to do.

Melina: Yes, settling back in.

Petrou: He doesn't mean that Melina!

[*Silence*]

[*PETROU drinks*]

Michalis: I need to rest.

Melina: Of course you do. It's been a long trip around all those islands. Come on Yannis, take his bags in.

[*PETROU looks at MELINA with some anger*]

Petrou: Let's have a drink Michalis.

[*PETROU offers MICHALIS a drink*]

Michalis: [*Stoically*] No.

[*PETROU pauses. He smiles*]

Petrou: Seeing you in the morning, Michalis, used to make my blood boil. Always at your mother's side; talking with that bitch Nan...

Melina: Yannis!

[*NANA smiles*]

Petrou: [*Pointing to birdtray*] Feeding your birds.

[*Silence*]

[*MELINA looks to birdtray, MICHALIS doesn't*]

Melina: We didn't forget it Michalis. Look...

Petrou: And now look at you; a fully-fledged off...Wait a minute! [*Turns to go up steps*] Wait till I get back!

[*PETROU goes off*]

[*MICHALIS sighs and sits. 'Nostalgia' begins. MICHALIS looks up*]

Michalis: I'm tired. We weren't allowed much sleep.

[*MELINA sits next to him*]

[*NANA comes on*]

Nana: Welcome home Michalis.

Melina: Nana!

[*MICHALIS doesn't move*]

Nana: I saw you get off the boat...Why are there so many soldiers coming to our small island Michalis?

Melina: Nana, his father will be back out in a minute.

Nana: The boat was full of soldiers Melina. They're down at the harbour. I only want to know why.

Melina: It's nothing to do with us. Do you want to spoil the homecoming?

Nana: If it spoils the homecoming to hear the truth it's not the truth that's to blame. [*Coming close to MICHALIS conspiratorially*] YOU know what I mean, Michalis: when you've been forced to live on a ledge high above a killer sea, you need to know what the next downpour of rain will do to your life.

[*NANA suddenly starts back*]

Nana: Tell him to take his cap off Melina. I can't see his eyes!

[*MELINA gets up angrily*]

Petrou: [*Off*] Present arms!

[*The sound of him drilling*]

Nana: [*Beginning to go*] Just remember this, Melina. The truth doesn't belong to you like your hotel or your son's homecoming. It's not there...

Petrou: [*Off*] Shoulder arms!

[*The sound of him drilling*]

Nana: ...just to make you happy in the morning. The truth is like this island. It belongs to us all!

[*NANA goes*]

[*PETROU comes out with a rifle on his shoulder. He comes down steps to MICHALIS. He present rifle to MICHALIS*]

Petrou: Here's a sign of the times, boy. How things have changed: at last I can show you this. A Lee Enfield 303. British. Feel it!

[*MICHALIS takes rifle without much enthusiasm*]

Melina: Yannis! Michalis is tired!

[*PETROU looks angry*]

[*MICHALIS offers rifle back*]

Petrou: [*Relaxing, taking rifle*] Later, then.

[*Pause*]

[*PETROU looks at birdtable, he smiles*]

Petrou: Shoulder arms!

[*PETROU drills then marches off up steps*]

[*Silence*]

[*MELINA looks closely at MICHALIS*]

Melina: Did they treat you well?

[*Pause*]

Michalis: I feel...um...we have to learn.

[*MELINA tips MICHALIS's cap back. MICHALIS quickly puts it back into place*]

Michalis: Don't mother!

Melina: I only wanted...

Michalis: I don't like.

Melina: ... to see your eyes...

Michalis: There's too much light.

[*Silence*]

Melina: Let's go in.

[*MICHALIS and MELINA stand*]

[*MICHALIS picks up bag. MELINA picks up tray... They go off up steps*]

Michalis: [*As they go off*] Can you change the music?

Melina: But it's your favourite!

[*Pause*]

[They go into the hotel]

[Music stops]

["Ela Agapi Mou" by Manos Tacticos begins]

[NANA comes on and sits defiantly on the steps]

[After a moment, PADDY MILANNE comes on struggling with a large suitcase. He speaks to someone following him]

[PADDY MILANNE is, in the main, a preoccupied man]

Paddy: I'm a democrat Sylv. A socialist and a democrat. And as such, as you know, I believe in the right of a man to his holiday. In fact, it's holidays that make democracies!

[He sees NANA]

Paddy: Like going to the theatre. In a democracy, you ought to be allowed, now and then, to forget the real world.

[He stops, puts down his case and turns to look back the way he came]

Paddy: But there has to be someone at work! To service the people who are taking the holidays!

[Pause]

Paddy: [To NANA] Hello. Do you speak English?

[NANA looks blank]

Paddy: Is this the hotel?

[NANA shrugs. PADDY looks up above steps]

Paddy: [Shouting over his shoulder] I've found it Sylv!

[SYLVIA struggles on with a large suitcase. She also has a handbag]

Sylvia: You and your crusades Paddy. You've landed us on an island full of soldiers. Where's the holiday in that?

[SYLVIA puts suitcase down]

Paddy: But we've arrived in the cradle of civilisation!

Sylvia: Well if this is the cradle of civilisation, there's a big fat sergeant in it.

Paddy: And we've come to look. To find out why.

Sylvia: That's not true, Paddy. You weren't expecting it to be an army barracks.

[Pause]

Paddy: It may be that from this very island, those first Greeks - the ones who gave us democracy - came. [Almost wistfully] It's like being born again as a couple of barbarians.

Sylvia: One, Paddy. Speak for yourself.

Paddy: [*To NANA, humorously*] You don't mind a couple of visiting barbarians do you? [*Pause*] You look like one yourself.

[*NANA shrugs*]

Sylvia: I've got to sit down before I collapse.

[*She takes a chair without help from PADDY*]

Paddy: I don't think that woman understand a word I'm saying.

[*SYLVIA sits*]

Sylvia: Why should she when she's Greek?

Paddy: How do you know that?

Sylvia: She's a tramp! Look at the way she's dressed. You wouldn't get a British tramp on a Greek island. Your tramps are your own.

[*SYLVIA dabs her face with her handkerchief. She then puts it on her head*]

Sylvia: I'm dying of exposure Paddy. See if you can get us a drink.

[*MICHALIS comes to the top of the steps. He is now in shirt sleeves but still wearing his cap. He starts as he sees PADDY and SYLVIA. He pauses for a moment looking bewildered*]

[*NANA looks at MICHALIS sadly*]

[*PADDY and SYLVIA look at MICHALIS for a second or two before he goes back into hotel*]

Sylvia: [*Unhappily*] Another one.

Paddy: What?

Sylvia: Another soldier, Paddy!

Paddy: That's not necessarily true. He could be a waiter.

Sylvia: A waiter! He was a soldier!

Paddy: [*Suddenly angry*] Why are you taking that tone with me! I've seen the soldiers. It offends me too. ME more than anyone.

Sylvia: So why did you bring us here?

Paddy: I didn't expect a battalion of the Greek army to be on the same boat as us.

Sylvia: They could be anywhere Paddy when they run the government.

[*PADDY jumps up angrily*]

Paddy: I have an obligation - as a socialist, as a democrat, as a trade unionist, as a councillor - you name it Sylv, as just a man who believes in holidays... I have a DUTY to use my holidays in a worthwhile way... If you're looking for the world you've got to come to these kind of places. On the other hand, rather than put us right in the middle of Athens where - well you know me, it could get us into trouble, something could have happened and I wouldn't be able to close my eyes to it - I thought we'd come here. We'd have, if you like, a bit of both - a bit of the fascism and a bit of the peace to investigate it. [*Pause, he goes to steps*] On the other hand, just look at it from the point of view of holidays. [*He taps the step with his foot. Smugly*] Look. Temple steps. Temple steps leading into a hotel. Where else but in Greece, where else but this tucked-away island of Greece would you get that?

Sylvia: Paddy, Barry Island would have done me.. They've got steps like that where they sell the candy-floss.

[*PADDY makes a dismissive noise*]

Paddy: I'll get you a drink and sign us in at the same time.

Sylvia: [*Sighing*] Thank god for that. I feel as if my whole body was melting in a chip pan. [*Pause*] I know! My fan! Where's my little fan?

Paddy: It's in your handbag.

[*SYLVIA digs into her handbag. She takes out a small, battery-operated fan*]

[*NANA looks at SYLVIA with surprise as SYLVIA operates the fan*]

[*PADDY goes up steps and almost bumps into PETROU who is coming out*]

[*PETROU now wears a peaked policeman's cap*]

Paddy: [*Slowly*] Ah! This...is...the...hotel?

Petrou: Hotel, yes. We were not...we did not know you come. [*Pause*] You stay here. We will make room.

Paddy: [*Surprised*] You...are...land...lord?

Petrou: I own hotel. Yes.

Paddy: But...[*To SYLVIA smugly*] The landlord is a policeman, Sylv.

[*Pause*]

[*He goes in*]

[*PETROU smiles at SYLVIA. He comes down steps towards NANA*]

Petrou: [*To NANA*] You miserable bitch. Go and get fucked somewhere will you? Get off my steps.

Nana: I want to see Michalis.

Sylvia: [*Smilingly, to PETROU*] It's such a lovely language. My husband says it's one of the oldest in the world. He knows a lot about the world.

Petrou: I sorry...I don't know much to speak...

Sylvia: You carry on. Don't mind me.

Petrou: You not speak the Greek?

Sylvia: Not an iota.

Petrou: It OK. I have to talk to poor lady?

Sylvia: You carry on love.

[*SYLVIA looks around her*]

Petrou: [*To NANA still calmly*] Right, come on. Go and fuck with the devil.

Sylvia: [*Seeing birdtable*] O-o, a birdtable!

Petrou: [*To NANA*] Michalis is a soldier now. There's no begging from soldiers.

Sylvia: [*Remembering something*] That sandwich!

[*She digs into her bag*]

Nana: I don't have to beg. I've got money.

[*SYLVIA takes out a sandwich wrapped in a serviette*]

Sylvia: I bought this on the boat and couldn't finish it.

[*She gets up and goes to birdtable*]

Petrou: You're a liar, Leros.

[*SYLVIA breaks up sandwich into small bits and puts them on table*]

Sylvia: I don't suppose they'll mind a bit of tuna.

[*NANA fumbles in her skirt. She takes out a coin and holds it up defiantly*]

[*PETROU snatches the coin from her*]

[*SYLVIA continues with the birdtable keeping her back to PETROU and NANA*]

[*PETROU looks quickly to SYLVIA*]

Petrou: [*Holding up coin*] A poxy drachma.

[*PETROU laughs loudly*]

[*SYLVIA turns very briefly to him with a smile*]

Petrou: [*Looking at coin*] This isn't yours.

Nana: [*Confused*] What?

Petrou: Whose head is on it?

Nana: But...

Petrou: It's the colonel's. The Prime Minister. If his head is on the coin, whose coin do you think it is? Yours or Colonel Papadopoulos's?

Sylvia: O-o-o-o, Papadropldoplepos. That's a word I recognise. Isn't that your Prime Minister? Mr. Papleoplepos?

Petrou: [*To SYLVIA*] No, no! Pa...pa...[*Pronounced ba ba*] do...pou... los [*Pronounced 'losh.'*] a great man.

Sylvia: I've seen photo's of him everywhere. He's got nice eyes. Like pools of tears.

[*PETROU smiles*]

[*SYLVIA looks off as if she's seen something*]

Petrou: [*To NANA*] It's the Colonel's drachma and he's lent it to me.

[*PADDY comes to top of steps. He carries a glass of water*]

Sylvia: [*To herself*] I can see a boat.

[*PETROU puts the coin in his pocket*]

[*NANA lets out a cry of injustice and grabs onto PETROU*]

[*PETROU pushes her off roughly*]

[*PADDY looks at this with displeasure*]

[*PETROU looks off at approaching boat*]

[*PADDY comes down steps and stands where NANA was sitting*]

[*NANA goes down steps and stands there looking lonely and isolated*]

Paddy: Sylvia.

[*SYLVIA goes to PADDY*]

Sylvia: Paddy, have you got that drink? I'm turning to liquid here.

[*SYLVIA takes the drink*]

Sylvia: There's a boat.

[*MICHALIS comes to the top of the steps*]

Nana: Michalis!

[*MICHALIS looks to sea*]

[*NANA looks forlorn*]

[*SYLVIA drinks water*]

Paddy: I'm inclined to say something Sylvia.

Petrou: What's that boat Michalis? It looks like a warship.

Michalis: It's a cruiser. It's called the Elli.

Sylvia: [*Finishing drink with a gasp*] I felt that go straight through to my back! I've got to sit now.

[*SYLVIA almost struggles to a chair*]

[*PADDY goes to her*]

[*MICHALIS takes PADDY's place on the steps*]

Michalis [*Bemused*] I can't understand where these people came from.

Paddy: [*Angrily but keeping his voice down*] I'm inclined to say that I don't see why I have to put up with...fascist tactics right before my eyes.

[*MICHALIS looks at PADDY sternly for an instant*]

Petrou: They come from the same boat as you. Why didn't you see them?

Sylvia: [*To PADDY*] Hear that?

Paddy: What?

Sylvia: The talk. The Greek. That's what you should be concerned with. You can almost decide for yourself what they're saying. To give the most benefit to the holiday.

Paddy: [*Ironically*] You mean if I wanted to I could imagine they were discussing the future of democracy in the world?

Petrou: [*About NANA*] Get rid of her Michalis.

Paddy: Like the old Greeks. In the old forum. Well I know they're not.

Sylvia: Of course they're not. They're probably deciding what we're going to have for tea.

Paddy: Because I saw the landlord hit the tramp.

[*MICHALIS comes to the bottom of the steps and a bit to the front*]

[*NANA looks more isolated at the back*]

Michalis: [*To PETROU*] Do you think we could arrest them for something?

[*NANA gasps and goes off*]

Sylvia: Paddy, what are you going to do? Arrest him? He's a policeman. Policemen are entitled to behave in a peculiar way according to the situation. You've never been a great lover of beggars in the past anyway.

Petrou: Don't be crazy Michalis. Think of the stories they'd take home with them then.

Paddy: OK Sylv. That's true. From a philosophical point of view, if you like, strictly speaking she's one of the lumpenproletariat. But that's alright in theory. In reality I'm more human than that.

Sylvia: Well be a bit more human to me Paddy Milanne and shut your mouth. Prove to me you haven't brought me, yet again, into danger on my holiday!

[*She turns away from him with anger*]

Petrou: What's on that boat Michalis?

[*PADDY sits by SYLVIA with a sigh*]

Paddy: That's a navy boat. [*To PETROU*] A...navy boat?

Petrou: Yes.

Paddy: Must be on manoeuvres.

Sylvia: You're so two faced Paddy.

Paddy: What now?

Petrou: The civilian boat brought your soldiers, Michalis, so what's that one bringing?

Sylvia: One minute you're about to report him to the United Nations and the next you're all lovey dovey asking him about boats!

Michalis: It's on manoeuvres.

Paddy: [*Gasps*] I know about boats! I was in the navy during the war!

Sylvia: Don't start talking about the war Paddy or we'll be here all day!

Paddy: I can say this: If it hadn't been for the war I wouldn't've known there was a world out there waiting for me. In war you get to see places you wouldn't normally see.

Sylvia: [*Ironically*] I suppose that's true. I spent four years on the inside of a cordite factory.

Petrou: Will it be stopping here?

Michalis: Overnight, yes.

Paddy: Shall I tell you something Sylvia?

[*MELINA comes to the top of the steps*]

Sylvia: Paddy, I have to listen to you 52 weeks a year. Now that I've come this far to be with the Greeks, I'd like to listen to them.

[*PADDY looks bitter*]

Petrou: Maybe they'll take that bitch Leros back with them when they leave.

Melina: Why is that boat coming here Michalis?

Petrou: Don't get involved with this Melina. I know what it's all about. Michalis is in charge now of two boats. You just make sure everything goes as smoothly as possible [*Indicating PADDY and SYLVIA*] And keep those two out of the way.

[*MELINA goes to MICHALIS*]

Melina: [*Sadly*] I didn't know you'd become so important Michalis. Changes happen so quickly these days.

[*MELINA puts an arm around him*]

Melina: Of course I'll help you.

Petrou: [*Impatiently*] Come on Michalis! We've got things to talk about.

[*PETROU goes off up steps*]

[*MICHALIS follows him off*]

Melina: [*To SYLVIA and PADDY*] We hope you will be very happy here. I am Mrs. Petrou. I own the hotel.

Sylvia: You speak good English.

Melina: You have to. It's the language of the Americans.

[*PADDY laughs*]

Paddy: [*Nudging SYLVIA*] I like that.

[*SYLVIA looks at PADDY with anger*]

Melina: If you need anything...

[*MELINA indicates hotel and goes off up steps*]

Sylvia: [*Angrily*] What right have you got laughing like that? She wasn't making a joke as far as I was aware of.

Paddy: How do you know?

Sylvia: How do you know she was? As far as I'm concerned I'm not prepared to take that chance. She didn't laugh; no nudge. And she's Greek. That's what you have to bear in mind. She's Greek.

[*Silence*]

Paddy: You know...your view of the world Sylvia...it's so carefree... uncluttered...black and white, sad or happy. No problems.

Sylvia: I know the world I live in. If I didn't I'd go mad.

[*Pause*]

Paddy: You know when I got sent home from the war? When I broke my skull?

Sylvia: You mean when you fell out of that window when you were drunk.

Paddy: Yes.

Sylvia: What do you want to go over all that for?

Paddy: I'm just thinking about it.. How old was I? 19? 20? I was a boy. My father beat me up.

[*Silence*]

[*SYLVIA looks to sea*]

Paddy: He beat me up.. For getting drunk in the war and coming home alive.

Sylvia: You made a holiday of the war Paddy. [*Pause*] He should have seen that you had a talent for holidays even in those days.

Paddy: Don't make a joke out of it.

Sylvia: [*Angrily*] I'm not making a joke! But do you think I want to sit here and hear about how all your friends died on the boat while you were in Sorrento? In hospital with a bandage around your head?

[*Silence*]

Paddy: The point is, what I'm saying is: life's not as clear-cut as you make it out to be. It was when he beat me up I became a socialist.

[*SYLVIA scoffs*]

Paddy: You can take that attitude but you think about it! It all fits. Because being a socialist isn't clear-cut either. Life is much more confusing than you make it out and you have to WORK to clear up the confusion.

Sylvia: I suppose you're going to tell me that's why you need a holiday. After all the work clearing up the confusion. Well let me tell you this: There's only one thing that needs clearing up here and that's whether I'm going to sleep out here under the stars tonight or in a bed where I belong!

[*PADDY gets up ill-humouredly*]

Paddy: I haven't signed us in yet.

Sylvia: While you're at it get us a parasol. My head's turning into a doughnut.

[*PADDY goes up steps*]

[*As PADDY reaches the top, PETROU comes out carrying a tray, with a jug of water and some glasses*]

Paddy: [*To PETROU*] Ex...cu...se me. H-a-a-ve you got an um...brella? Par..a..sol?

[*PADDY mimes putting up an umbrella. PETROU points for him to go into the hotel. PADDY goes*]

[*PETROU comes down steps and puts tray on table. PETROU smiles at SYLVIA*]

Petrou: [*Casually*] Tonight, festival.

Sylvia: I beg you pardon.

Petrou: Tonight! Boat come. [*Points off*] People come here. Tonight. March in festival for saint.

Sylvia: Tonight? A festival?

Petrou: For island saint.

Sylvia: Tonight?

Petrou: Tonight.

[*PETROU begins to go off up steps*]

Sylvia: [*After PETROU*] When tonight?

[*SYLVIA pours herself a glass of water. She drinks it straight down*]

[*PADDY comes down steps carrying a large, dilapidated sun-umbrella*]

Sylvia: Paddy, there's a festival tonight.

Paddy: What?

Sylvia: The landlord just told me there's going to be a festival tonight.

[*PADDY opens the umbrella and moves the tray from the centre of the table*]

Paddy: A festival? What kind of festival? There's no bloody hole in this table! There's no way I can see of getting it to stand up.

Sylvia: Give it to me. I'll hold it.

[*PADDY props the umbrella next to SYLVIA*]

Paddy: What festival?

Sylvia: The landlord just told me that people from that boat are going to march tonight in a festival to celebrate the saint of the island. A carnival Paddy. Floats, the lot.

[*PADDY looks suddenly unburdened*]

Paddy: You see?

[*Pause*]

Sylvia: What?

Paddy: We were being too gloomy. In Greece, I believe, there's always hope. It's in their language. You can find it out from their words. Only this morning I was reading a book about their words. I'll give you an example. ANTHROPOS. Very ancient. What do you think it means.

Sylvia: I don't know.

[*PADDY is next to SYLVIA*]

Paddy: It means: "He who looks upwards". Who do you think it refers to?

Sylvia: [*Sighing. A little brow-beaten*] I don't know. The working class?

Paddy: Don't be stupid! MAN! It means MAN!

Sylvia: [*Angrily*] I'm not stupid Paddy Milanne. Not everyone looks upwards. A lot of people look down on others. Half the time I'm looking up at you while you're looking down on me. What's man got to do with anything?

Paddy: You're missing the point of what I'm saying. Obviously, when they made that word they were living in times when everybody looked up TOGETHER. That's the beauty of the Greeks isn't it? This is where justice came from. They've got a natural kind of equality. They're all looking up. There was a slogan on the wall in Pireaus. I asked what it meant. We got on the boat and I forgot to tell you. Do you know what is said? It said: "Greek justice is and always will be the best justice that ever existed in human society." See? You can't keep it down. Even the army can't do that. This is where it came from.

[*PADDY kisses SYLVIA on the head. He begins to go up steps*]

Sylvia: Where are you going now?

Paddy: I haven't signed in yet!

Sylvia: Well take the suitcases.

[*PADDY comes back quickly for the suitcases*]

Sylvia: And slow down or you'll have a haemorrhage.

[*PADDY gets suitcases and goes off up steps with them*]

[*After a moment, MELINA comes down steps*]

Melina: [*Coming to SYLVIA*] Hello.

Sylvia: Oh, hello Mrs. Petrou.

Melina: My husband is helping your husband with the room. I thought this would be a good time to speak.

Sylvia: I can't get over your English. It's almost better than mine!

Melina: I was in America sometime. In war and after. [*Pause*] We hope you will enjoy yourselves.

Sylvia: I expect we will. It's nice and quiet here.

Melina: We do not have many tourists. It is off main sea route.

[*MELINA sits*]

Sylvia: So that accounts for it! It's a pity. With the festival tonight.

Melina: [*After a pause*] I don't understand. What festival?

Sylvia: Your husband just told me there was a festival tonight. The people from the boat celebrating the saint.

[*Silence*]

[*MELINA thinks. She looks angry*]

Melina: I see. [*Short pause*] Tell me, why have you come to our island?

Sylvia: You mean on holiday?

Melina: Yes.

Sylvia: It's Paddy. He's always dragging me half way across the world. Mind you, it gives him prestige. I should be proud of Paddy. He's got positions. [*Short pause*] I say things like: "What do you want to go to these...um..mysterious, you know, extreme places for?" He says: "I don't want to go down the same old track as the Teagues or the Crowleys." - they're neighbours. He says: "I'm looking for the world and I won't find it in Benidorm." Me, give me a bit of sun, a sand dune and a good thriller and I've found it. [*Pause*] He gets dramatic. He says: "If we end up in one of those transit camps on the Mediterranean" - that's what he calls the Costa del Sol! "Then I might as well be dead." I say: "You're exaggerating a bit now Paddy" and he says: "The cup of my life is not full and it's never going to get full from empty teapots."

[*PADDY comes to the top of the step*]

Paddy: Come here Sylv.

Sylvia: What do you want now Paddy? You're always on the go.

Paddy: Come and look at our room. You won't believe your eyes.

Sylvia: Why won't I?

Paddy: Because you'd only expect to find such a place in a book on mythology.

[*SYLVIA gets up with a sigh*]

Sylvia: Let's hope we don't have Jason and the Argonatus coming in in the middle of the night!

[*SYLVIA gives the shade to MELINA. Goes up steps and off with PADDY*]

[*MICHALIS comes to top of steps. He is in shirt sleeves. He still wears his cap*]

Melina: Michalis, come and sit.

[*MICHALIS sits by his mother*]

Melina: Is anything...wrong?

[*Silence*]

Melina: I can tell when my baby's hurt.

Michalis: If you think there's something wrong with me mother then you've misunderstood things.

Melina: I meant...

Michalis: In Athena there is a house on Bouboulinas Street. It has a terrace and beneath the terrace there is a motor cycle. [*Pause*] Traitors are brought onto the terrace. They are asked to repent and denounce their communistic ideas.

[*MELINA looks perplexed*]

Michalis: Many do quietly on the terrace. We bring them back into the national community. If they don't repent, the motor cycle is started up. Sometimes it stands there with its engine screaming all night until finally, by the morning, there is silence. From the terrace and from beneath it. [*Short pause*] So yes, there are some things wrong, but that is what is being done to put them right.

[*Silence*]

Melina: Why has that ship come to our island?

Michalis: I've explained. It's on manoeuvres.

[*Pause*]

Melina: Then why did your father tell the tourists that there was going to be a festival tonight?

[*Pause*]

Michalis: [*A little clumsily*] Because there will be some noise.

Melina: But it will be quite clear to them that it's not a festival. They'll be able to see.

Michalis: No mother, there'll be the curfew.

[*Pause*]

Melina: [*Bemused*] But why would anybody have a festival and a curfew that stops people seeing it?

Michalis: Mother, I don't know. Please, leave me alone... I've got so much on my mind.

[*MICHALIS begins to get up*]

Melina: [*Pulling at him*] Wait, Michalis. Please, treat me with respect. I am your mother. If I don't know what's going on how can I speak to these people? How can I help you?

[*MICHALIS gets up*]

Michalis: Make sure they are in bed as soon as possible after the curfew. There will be patrols.

[*MELINA gets up*]

Melina: Do you know Michalis, since you went away hardly a bird has visited us. It seems as if all the natural life has gone from the island.

[*She goes to the birdtable*]

Melina: But look. This morning it was empty. Now it's full as if the bread had fallen from the sky. And you are home.

Michalis: I'd better go down to the harbour. They'll need me.

Melina: Understand this, Michalis. You're still a boy. It takes years to learn order; to learn to keep things in place to give ourselves the

calm we need. Just putting on a uniform won't give you that. I
have learnt. I understand. And so I can help. And you must
understand that. [*Pause*] The tourists have been travelling all day.
They're tired. They'll be in bed.

[*MICHALIS goes off*]

[*Lights down*]

Scene Five

Scene: *Evening.*

There is quiet Bouzouki music playing throughout most of the scene.

*MELINA is laying the table. The olives have been replaced. She puts a
variety of bowls, containing different dishes, to dip into, onto the table.
She goes back up the steps.*

*MELINA comes back out after a moment or two with a tray on which
there are two tin jugs of rezina, a jug of water and some glasses. She
puts cloths over the food. She stands still for a moment. She goes back up
steps and off.*

After a moment, SYLVIA comes on leaning very heavily on NANA.

*SYLVIA is a little out of breath. As they reach the tables, SYLVIA almost
falls into chair.*

Sylvia: [*To NANA*] Thank you dear. I don't know what I would have
done on that hill if I hadn't met you. I don't care if you are a
tramp. Sit down love.

[*SYLVIA indicates to NANA to sit. SYLVIA breathes deeply for a second
or two*]

[*NANA sits*]

Sylvia: That bloody Paddy. If it was left up to him I could have died
on the cobbles. Paddy looks into everything. Especially dark little
bars where you don't know what could be lurking in the corner.
Like that Homer's Cave. And especially when he's angry. It was
the same in Athens. Down all the dingy streets. Looking into those
kind of places. There it was because he thought we weren't going
to get a boat. Now it's because we couldn't get on the harbour. I
told him, I said: "I suppose they're preparing for the festival. They
don't want busy bodies snooping round watching people putting
on their costumes." We should be grateful that there were so few
soldiers in sight.

[*PETROU comes to the top of the steps. He looks at NANA with
incredulity. He is unseen by the two*]

Sylvia: I don't know what I'm talking to you for. You can't understand a word I'm saying. Never mind. [*Looking at NANA closely*] What about [*She mimics eating with her fingers, i.e. dipping her fingers into the food*] food? [*She mimics eating with her fingers again*] Food.

[*NANA looks at the food. She points to it. She goes to lift the cloth to show SYLVIA*]

[*PETROU comes down the steps quickly*]

Petrou: Get your filthy, fucking hands away from the food! Christ!

[*PETROU smiles at SYLVIA reassuringly. He takes NANA's hand and stops her from touching the cloth*]

[*SYLVIA smiles*]

Petrou: [*To NANA*] I thought I warned you. You could be dealt with very severely already for stealing the Prime Minister's money.

Nana: I went to Mr. Metaxis's shop and told him what you said. He laughed. I asked if I could see some of his coins. He laughed again. Then he placed a few of very small value on his counter. Some had the king's head on them and some had the head of Papadopoulos. I asked him who the coins belonged to. He leaned right over the counter into my face and said: "Me." But only until he gives it to someone else. The only thief is the one who takes it as you took mine. The people on this island are neighbours. They exchange coins as neighbours. If you haven't got a coin in your pocket you haven't got a neighbour. The drachma is not important in itself. It's how it's used. If you take it away you throw people out. If you give it back, you give them communion. That's the way it is.

Petrou: Did you say all this to Mr. Metaxis?

Nana: Yes.

Petrou: And what did he say?

[*Short pause*]

Nana: He threw me out.

Petrou: I warn you Leros. A time is coming when there will be no more throwing out.

[*Silence*]

Sylvia: I love to hear you speak your Greek. It adds flavour to the air. Excuse me Mr Petrou [*She indicates food*] is that the food?

[*PETROU lifts cloth*]

Petrou: Here is food. Food for all.

Sylvia: It's all ready! That's nice. [*She breathes deep*] We had a lovely day, me and Paddy. [*She looks around her*] It could be paradise this place. We had a little walk. Nothing too much; not too far. Lots of stops. A nice little gallivant. It's lovely in the evening now it's cool.

[*PETROU smiles at her politely*]

Petrou: [*To NANA*] If you refuse to go...

Nana: The woman invited me to sit at her table.

[*PETROU goes up steps and off angrily*]

Sylvia: I'm a bit peckish now I must say. We had a bit of food dinner time. I brought a few tins with me from home. You never know when you come on these foreign holidays.

[*PADDY comes on from left. He looks pre-occupied. He stops. He looks with distaste at NANA*]

Paddy: [*To SYLVIA*] Why didn't you wait?

[*SYLVIA cranes her neck around to look at PADDY*]

Sylvia: Oh!, finished your guzzling have you?

Paddy: Why is that woman at the table Sylv? Is she eating with us?

Sylvia: I don't know why you bother to come all this way. You may as well have spent a fortnight down the Legion.

Paddy: The tramp shouldn't be at the table.

[*PADDY goes to NANA and puts a coin on the table before her*]

Sylvia: She helped me up that hill! She's having a rest.

Nana: [*Sadly. Picking up coin*] I know what this is for.

Sylvia: Listen to her Paddy. How sad her words sound. You've hurt her now. Is that your socialism?

Nana: This morning Petrou took a coin from me to steal my communion. Now you GIVE me a coin to do the same.

[*NANA puts coin back on table*]

Sylvia: She's too proud for charity Paddy!

Paddy: My socialism...[*Stung*] Whatever you want to call it, is a bit more complicated. Nobody ANYwhere has tramps at their table. You of all people...Christ, you never wanted a dog because dogs are dirty!

Sylvia: There's a difference between a dog and a woman!

Paddy: Yes! A woman can decide for herself what she wants to be; what she wants...if she wants to be a tramp or...

Sylvia: Or what?

[*Silence*]

[*PADDY goes to the left and looks off*]

Paddy: I don't want to argue Sylvia...

[*SYLVIA scoffs*]

Paddy: I've discovered something. [*Pause. Calmly*] As we walked down the hill...when we could see the harbour and the small bay, it occurred to me...the boat went down in a place like this.

Sylvia: [*Sighing*] Are you thinking again about the boat in the war Paddy where all your friends were killed?

Paddy: Of course. It went down in a small bay here in Greece. One of these hundreds of islands. I could feel myself being lifted almost from the cares of the world. As a sign of respect. [*Pause*] The whole island suddenly became like a memorial for those dead boys.

[*SYLVIA makes a silent gesture as if to say: "He's off again"*]

Paddy: Do you remember when we were in Paris?

Sylvia: How could I forget? I nearly got run over by an armoured car.

Paddy: Yes. Only not the noise in the street: the noise of revolt. When we went to that graveyard. Like a miniature city - almost Greek come to think of it - decked with flowers. Do you remember the beauty of that peace? That's what it felt like going down the hill. Almost like a two minutes silence. As if on this island should be a continuous two minutes silence. And do you know what Sylv? Look at a map. The island is shaped like a wreath.

[*MELINA comes to top of steps*]

Melina: Nana!

[*They all look at MELINA*]

Melina: [*Coming down steps*] You must leave the table Nana.

Nana: Let me stay...or let me stay on the steps...if I go...we will lose Melina. You and I.

Melina: I can't help it. If you stay...

[*MELINA puts hands on NANA*]

[*SYLVIA looks upset*]

Melina: Times are difficult enough without the tensions you create Nana.

[*NANA gets up*]

Sylvia: [*Aside to PADDY*] See what you've done? Always got to have your own way. Paddy the bully!

[*MELINA leads NANA off*]

Paddy: No Sylvia. I'm taking a balanced view.

Sylvia: Oh! balanced on a bottle of wine, I suppose!

Paddy: I was feeling sad! I had a drink.

Sylvia: One of the few things I like about this place is that so far there's no sign of hooliganism. Except for you!

Paddy: Well if I'm a hooligan, you're a hypocrite!

Sylvia: I may BE a hypocrite Milanne, but I am not a traitor!

[*PADDY is stung*]

Sylvia: I didn't go into that Homer's Cave leaving anybody on the street like you deserted me.

Paddy: I had a drink...

Sylvia: I know. That's what I'm talking about. And don't you know you can get double dehydration in the heat you get in this country? We're not home now. I can't look after you like I can there.

Paddy: Your trouble, Sylv, is you bring with you all the tensions of home life. You don't know the first rule of holidaying.

Sylvia: Don't give me a sermon Paddy Milanne. I'm an expert on holidays. I've lived my life for them. [*Pause*] One thing: [*She gets up and points to banner*] You want to find out what that says. It could be a warning of some kind.

Paddy: It's probably got something to do with the festival.

[*Pause*]

Sylvia: [*Hopefully*] Do you think so?

[*Pause*]

Sylvia: [*Going to PADDY*] It would be lovely if we could make this holiday...a perfect one.

Paddy: We will.

[*Silence*]

Sylvia: Paddy, you don't think it WAS this island do you?

Paddy: I wouldn't've brought us here if I did.

Sylvia: So why think it?

[*MELINA comes back on*]

Sylvia: Oh, excuse me Mrs Petrou. We were just wondering [*Indicates banner*] What does that say?

Melina: [*Smiling*] It says: welcome home Officer Petrou. Michalis. My son..He has been away at Athena. Training to be an officer.

Sylvia: It must be like welcoming home a returning hero.

[*PADDY looks unhappy*]

Melina: Yes.

Sylvia: You must be very proud.

Melina: I am.

[*MELINA goes off up steps*]

[*PADDY moves off to right*]

Paddy: [*Unenthusiastically*] Not only do we arrive on the day of a major festival but on the day of a major homecoming as well.

[*Pause*]

Paddy: You know what these Greeks are like for homecomings.

Sylvia: Not really, Paddy.

Paddy: The Trojan War.

Sylvia: Paddy, why don't you take your mind off war? You'll drive yourself...

Paddy: [*Almost tearfully*] When they put me in that council chair, they did it because...TO SOME EXTENT because they regarded me as...as a man who...as maybe even a hero...Christ!

[*He rushes off*]

Sylvia: Where are you going Paddy? Tea's nearly ready! [*Pause*] Oh, god!

[*Silence*]

[*After a moment, MELINA comes down steps with a tray. On it are three glasses and ouzo*]

Melina: Oh, your husband has gone?

Sylvia: He's gone. He's upset again.

Melina: It is a pity. I have brought a drink for us. Some ouzo. [*Puts tray on table*] It is good for evening. Gives an appetite. Will he return your husband?

[*MELINA pours drink*]

Sylvia: He'll be back. It's just his war wound playing up.

[*MELINA pours water into SYLVIA's glass. SYLVIA looks with interest as the drink turns milky. SYLVIA takes glass*]

Sylvia: Ta, love. I'll just have a sip, see what it tastes like. [*She sips*] M-m-m-m, it tastes like Pernod. That's one of Paddy's favourites.

Melina: What is the war wound?

Sylvia: It's not one like that. You could say the wound was the war itself. The ship he was supposed to be on got blown up. Somewhere among these islands. Everybody on board was killed. They'd left Paddy behind in Sorrento because he'd got drunk and fallen out of a window. When he woke up in the hospital, he said, he thought he was in heaven! You know what those Italians are like for putting angels on ceilings! The trouble is, once a man's been in a war he's forever a soldier. Paddy won't let it lie.

[*SYLVIA takes a drink*]

Sylvia: M-m-m-m. All I'm waiting for now is to see the procession and that will have made my day.

Melina: What is this?

Sylvia: The procession? You know, the people from the boat.

Melina: Ah! But you will not see it.

Sylvia: Why not?

Sylvia: Because of the curfew.

Sylvia: [*Disappointed*] Oh, you've got one here. Oh, well. [*Pause*] We thought the one in Athens was just because it's a big city. [*Pause*] Mind you, when you hear about curfews it makes you think of those terrible countries in Africa where people get murdered in their sleep and gangs of drunken soldiers race around shooting anything that moves. I must say, in Athens it was quiet at night. That's one thing I long for. Where we live, there's no respect for day or night. Just the other day - I'm such a nervous thing - I was going over to the shop- I'd run out of something or the other. I came round this corner and a big, big black man came up to me. I thought: "My god, I'm going to be robbed!" I don't suppose you've got any here. They're our greatest enemy. Robbers.

Melina: With us it's the communists.

Sylvia: [*Surprised*] Communists? It doesn't seem like a country where you'd have a lot of communists.

Melina: That is because we have the curfew. It is enforced strictly.

[*SYLVIA looks anxious*]

Sylvia: Yes, I suppose that's it. Your enemies are worse at night. You can always tell them with us - they're like big muscle-bound apes. Anyway, this one rushes up to me and says: "Hey woman!" I thought: "This country's finished. There was a time when you'd never talk to a woman like that." He said: "Can you give me some change for the telephone box?" Well I wasn't going to show him my purse and let him rob it off me. So I said: "I'm sorry love, I'm only going for a walk." He seemed to go berserk! Rushing here and there. But there was nobody around. So then he went into the box. He was talking so loud I could hear him. He wanted to make a 'phone call through the operator and she must have said he could if he put some money in. Well, he didn't have any change. I thought she would have told him about transfer charges but she must have been able to tell he was black. There's a lot of people round these days thinking: "Why should you help those who don't help themselves? Even God wouldn't." So then he smashed the telephone into the window, smashed the glass, cut himself, left blood everywhere for some unsuspecting person to see and started yelling and screaming like some caged gorilla. I just ran off. I got home and sat and thought. If you want my opinion, people have got the wrong end of the stick. They'd let him get away with that because he's black. That's racialist. It would be racialist for me not to want to punish him with my thoughts. I saw it and I go by what I see.

Melina: I think sometimes that people should not go by what they see.

Sylvia: That's a funny thing to say. That's like saying that sometimes people should be blind.

Melina: There are those with power who put before our eyes pictures that are meant to hide the truth. The communists do that. We would be better off blind than to believe in the pictures.

Sylvia: Well, everybody's got their point of view, love, but as far as I'm concerned, I'd rather give up looking at all the pictures in the world than give up my eyesight. [*Pause*] Anyway, it's a pity we won't see the festivities.

Melina: One day we will not need the curfew. We have to go along with these things for the sake of the country. We do not like it.

[*PADDY comes on. He looks relaxed. Even a little happy*]

Melina: We have a saying here in Greece: "When the streets are quiet, the world is asleep."

[*PADDY stops to listen to the woman. He seems almost smug*]

Sylvia: That's exactly what I've been saying There's nothing worse than the noise people make coming home from the pub. And then playing their music till the early hours. If the curfew stops that then I'm all for it.

[*Pause*]

Melina: No. The saying means: When people stop discussing things in public, then we stop progress in the world. That is anathema to Greeks. But, sometimes, progress must be halted so that people can be protected.

Paddy: Hear! Hear!

Sylvia: [*Turning to see PADDY*] Paddy. Are you alright love?

Paddy: Don't worry about me. What's this about a curfew?

Sylvia: [*Unhappily*] Oh, they've got a curfew here too.

[*PADDY sits by SYLVIA. SYLVIA gives him drink*]

Paddy: [*Pleasantly*] Listen. I've got men in work who've never been nearer to a curfew than a shift-hooter! Men who could put their knowledge of the world on a time card. There are answers to things I want to know that they don't even know have got questions. That's why they holiday in Bournemouth and we holiday with the curfew! So cheer up!

Melina: [*Getting up*] We must eat!

[*MELINA goes off up steps*]

Sylvia: Good, I'm starving.

Paddy: [*Conspiratorially*] Anyway, Sylv. You said it yourself. How many people at home would like a curfew. To keep the riff-raff off the streets. It would be easier to count those who wouldn't.

[*SYLVIA locks her arm in PADDY's, gives him a smile and rests her head on his shoulder*]

[*The tune "Ela Agapi Mou" on bouzouki begins in the hotel*]

[*MELINA, MICHALIS and PETROU come down the steps*]

[*MICHALIS is in shirt sleeves with his cap on*]

[*PETROU still wears his police clothes with no cap*]

[*MELINA takes cloths off food*]

[*PETROU puts an arm around MICHALIS's shoulder to try and get him to dance*]

Petrou: Come on Michalis! Dance!

[*MICHALIS after taking a few steps, stops*]

Petrou: Tell him Melina! He won't dance!

Melina: Leave him alone Yannis, he doesn't want to.

Michalis: [*Complainingly*] I'm tired Papa!

Sylvia: It looks as if they're squabbling now!

Melina: Mr Petrou wants Michalis to dance but the boy is tired.

[*PETROU grunts and sits*]

[*MELINA puts glasses in front of all*]

Sylvia: [*Humorously*] I get the same with Paddy!

[*PADDY gives her a smile and a playful dig*]

[*PETROU dips into food with his fingers*]

[*MICHALIS does the same and sits*]

[*SYLVIA looks suddenly horrified*]

Sylvia: [*Aside to PADDY*] What are they doing Paddy?

Paddy: Eating. Look.

[*PADDY dips into food with his fingers*]

[*SYLVIA looks at him horrified*]

Sylvia: Paddy! How can you do it?

Paddy: Because they're doing it.

[*MELINA sits. She begins to eat*]

Sylvia: [*Under her breath to PADDY*] I'm not going to do it! That man has got a mouthful of spit. [*PETROU*] I'd rather starve! What if I hadn't brought those tins?

[*They all eat except SYLVIA*]

Petrou: [*To SYLVIA*] You eat. Come!

[*PETROU passes a bowl of food he's dipped into, to PADDY, who passes it to SYLVIA*]

Sylvia: I'm alone. I can see it now. Are you going to help me Paddy?

[*PADDY looks dismayed*]

Paddy: [*Politely to PETROU*] She's not hungry. She'll have wine.

[*PETROU hands PADDY the jug, shrugging*]

[*PADDY fills SYLVIA's glass. He hands it to her*]

[*SYLVIA takes a drink. Her face twists up*]

Sylvia: [*Quietly but urgently to PADDY*] Paddy!

Paddy: [*A little impatiently*] What!

Sylvia: I'm finished.

Paddy: [*Angrily*] What do you mean?

Sylvia: I'm finished as a tourist on this island! The wine tastes like metal cleaner!

Paddy: You'll get used to it!

[*PADDY sips his rezina*]

Sylvia: No I won't because I'm not going to touch it again! That's it! That's my holiday ruined.

Paddy: [*Almost panicking*] What do you want me to do?

Sylvia: You're the great crusader!

[*PADDY looks lost*]

Petrou: [*Speaking with a mouthful of food*] I think the woman is giving the man a pain where he shits!

[*PETROU laughs alone*]

[*SYLVIA turns to PADDY. She pulls him to her so that she can speak into his ear*]

Sylvia: Listen to that! It's revolting!

Paddy: What is?

Sylvia: That man speaking!

[*NANA comes on slowly across the front. She is carrying a begging bowl*]

[*Everyone at the table stops eating*]

[*MELINA looks at NANA with annoyance*]

[*SYLVIA looks at NANA with pity and fearful expectation*]

[*PADDY looks at NANA with disbelief*]

[*MICHALIS looks at NANA emptily and coldly*]

[*PETROU looks at NANA with outrage*]

Petrou: Melina! There's no safety from this woman! Send her away!

Melina: Come here Nana.

[*NANA moves to table. She calmly puts a hand into the food*]

Petrou: [*Rising noisily*] Melina!

[*NANA eats*]

Sylvia: [*Turning away with a groan of disgust*] God, Paddy!

Melina: Nana! Just give me your bowl.

[*NANA gives MELINA her bowl. MELINA puts food in it*]

Paddy: Now you know what I was talking about.

Sylvia: What you were talking about when?

Paddy: When I said people don't have tramps at the table.

Sylvia: [*Harshly*] You're contradicting yourself aren't you Paddy? I would have thought it was so different as to make your holiday.

Paddy: If anyone's contradicting themselves, you're the one who wanted her to stay. Now look at you!

Sylvia: Paddy, I make no bones about where I stand. For years I learnt manners - how to use a knife and fork. I believe in table-cloths!   And serviettes. You put a hand near the food in my father's house and he'd slice it off. I've never made any bones about that. No one can say that they don't know what I'm saying. All I'm looking for is a holiday!

[*NANA takes her bowl and eats from it without moving*]

[*PETROU looks at her threateningly*]

[*Lights down*]

[*END OF PART ONE*]

Part Two

Scene One

Scene: *Later. Just before curfew hour.*

A bright, brash light comes out of the hotel, flooding over the steps. Bouzouki music is heard playing quite loud. The tables have been cleared.

SYLVIA is sitting alone looking off apprehensively.

MELINA comes down steps.

Melina: You should go in Mrs. Milanne.

Sylvia: [*Turning to MELINA*] No, I'll have to wait for Paddy. He's like an over-grown boy. If I go to bed without him he's bound to get into trouble.

Melina: It's nearly ten o'clock. Where did he go?

Sylvia: You don't need to ask. That Homer's Cave. I just hope he comes back before the curfew. [*Pause*] He always leaves me sitting alone.

Melina: [*Looking off*] Men live in a world of their own.

Sylvia: I suppose we have to put up with it. [*Pause*] Especially when you think it's the world we live in too!

[*SYLVIA gives a little, nervous laugh*]

[*Siren sounds loudly*]

[*SYLVIA jumps up, startled*]

[*The music stops suddenly and most of the light goes. The light that's left is tinged with reds and greens*]

Sylvia: [*As the siren sounds. Shouting to be heard*] Paddy! [*The siren stops*]

Sylvia: [*Shouting*] Paddy!

[*MELINA comes to SYLVIA. She holds her*]

Melina: Ssssh! You must be quiet!

[*SYLVIA looks at MELINA with terror*]

Melina: We must go in.

[*They go up steps*]

[*SYLVIA stands at the top almost out of sight*]

[*There is some distant gunfire*]

[*SYLVIA bites her hand*]

[*PADDY comes on from the left. He is drunk though not rolling. He crosses and goes up the steps*]

Sylvia: You've got no consideration! What if you'd been arrested?

Paddy: Who's going to arrest me? [*Angrily*] I AM ME!

Sylvia: Didn't you hear that shot?

Paddy: That could've been the start of the festival. If they've got a festival there's not going to be much interest in the curfew. D'you know how I know?

[*SYLVIA goes off*]

Paddy: Because there's hardly any interest in the festival!

[*PADDY goes off*]

[*After a moment NANA slouches on. She sits on the steps*]

[*Soon, MICHALIS comes quickly to the top of the steps. He is straightening his uniform. He is in a state of near panic*]

Michalis: Leave the steps bitch!

Nana: [*Hurt*] Why?

Michalis: You're breaking the curfew.

Nana: How can I break the curfew if I'm a bitch? Dogs don't break the curfew. I see them scavenging at night.

Michalis: Leave the steps!

[*NANA gets up. She begins to go*]

Michalis: No wait!

[*He looks up above steps*]

Michalis: Go to my mother.

Nana: Why?

Michalis: Tell her I sent you.

[*MICHALIS moves towards NANA who backs off cowering*]

[*NANA suddenly hurries off*]

Michalis: Wait!

[*MICHALIS starts after her then stops. He gasps and goes off another way*]

[*Lights down*]

Scene Two

Scene: *Night*

There is little light tinged with reds and greens.

PETROU can be heard trying drunkenly and wildly to hum the tune of

"Nostalgia" from inside the hotel. This continues on and off throughout the scene. (Except when he comes out).

There is the sound of many people marching. The sound of metal like chains.

A motorbike engine runs getting louder and then diminishing and then louder again as if somebody is riding up and down a line.

The occasional bark of a dog.

The sound of orders shouted.

The general noise gets louder: i.e. closer.

NANA suddenly rushes on. She seems confused. She stops centrally for a moment. She goes to the steps.

Nana: The monsters!

[*NANA looks up above steps*]

Nana: Melina! They've stolen our island!

[*NANA sits on top step*]

[*MELINA comes out*]

Melina: [*With loud whisper*] Nana! are you mad!

Nana: Listen!

Melina: Go away!

[*MELINA takes hold of NANA roughly and pulls her up*]

Nana: Don't you want to know what it is?

[*MELINA pushes NANA*]

Nana: Don't you want to see what your son's brought to the island?

Melina: [*Going off with NANA*] It's his WORK!

[*They go off*]

[*PADDY comes out*]

Sylvia: [*Just off*] Paddy, come in!

Paddy: I want to see it!

Sylvia: [*Off*] You're breaking the curfew!

Paddy: Firstly, I've told you...no...don't you know by now that I will NOT be bullied? You have to stand up to these people. There are no curfews in civilisation. How do you think THIS country was civilised in the first place? [*Short pause*] Pericles! He would have stood on steps just like these...

[*SYLVIA has come to PADDY's side*]

Sylvia: [*Fearfully*] What's that noise?

Paddy: The festival. The process...

Sylvia: Not THAT noise! Paddy, I'm scared.

Paddy: [*Listening*] It's going round the back...

[*PADDY begins to go down steps*]

Sylvia: [*Terrified*] PADDY!

Paddy: I'll go and find out what it is!

[*PADDY goes off*]

[*The sound of PETROU's singing gets louder*]

[*SYLVIA goes in*]

[*PETROU comes to top of steps. He's very drunk*]

Petrou: Tonight!

[*MELINA comes back on.. She rushes up steps*]

Melina: Yannis! Get in!

[*MELINA pushes him off*]

Petrou: Uh?...oh!...

[*The noise reaches a climax*]

[*After a moment, SYLVIA comes to top of steps. She is crying*]

[*After a moment, PADDY comes on. He looks a little puzzled*]

Sylvia: Paddy!

Paddy: [*Climbing steps*] That was a bloody funny festival!

Sylvia: I'll never ever come on holiday with you again!

[*PADDY goes off*]

[*SYLVIA follows him*]

[*MICHALIS comes on. He stands centrally for a moment. He looks above steps, pauses and goes off again*]

[*Lights down*]

Scene Three

Scene: *Morning*

NANA is standing centrally, crying like a lost child.

MELINA comes to top of steps. She looks tired.

Melina: Why are you crying Nana?

[*Pause*]

Nana: When your husband stole my coin, what could I do to get it back?

Melina: When did he steal your coin?

[*Pause*]

Nana: All I could do is ask for it. And keep asking.

Melina: Is that why you're crying? I'll give you a coin.

Nana: Keep asking for it back every moment of his day until he couldn't sleep because of me. Then he would have to give me my coin or...

[*MELINA yawns*]

Melina: Nana, I didn't sleep much...

Nana: But still they came! [*Pause*] I could think: give up the coin it's stolen...

Melina: Yes! Give it up...

Nana: [*Getting more excited*] Is it worth putting my life in danger?

Melina: [*With incredulity*] Your life!

Nana: But what do I think when they've stolen my island? [*Pointing at MELINA*] Or if they'd stolen my son!

Melina: Nana!

Nana: When the schoolmaster went we could pretend he'd gone to work in Athens. Because we never saw them kill him...

Melina: [*Angrily*] Who?...

Nana: And when Michalis went to Athens we could pretend it was part of his education. But now I've seen what they're doing. How they're trying to turn our beautiful island into a rock for crows.

[*Silence*]

[*MELINA goes to NANA*]

Melina: Tell me what you saw.

[*NANA holds onto MELINA*]

Nana: Let me in, Melina. The island was once like a large family and I had a home. People were happy and strong - they believed in themselves. THEN I had a home. Now people are afraid. They will use me to get rid of their fear.

Melina: There! You see? It's you who's afraid! You're misinterpret...

Nana: [*Angrily*] Ask Michalis who those people were and where they were going. Or being taken!

Melina: [*Offended*] I will not! It's his...

Nana: [*Mimicking MELINA*] Work...

Melina: Career! [*Pause. Calmer*] How could we possibly know what the army are up to?

Nana: Send me away and you'll see!

[*Pause*]

Melina: You'd better come in. But don't speak about these things again. And don't let Mr. Petrou see you.

[*Lights down*]

Scene Four

Scene: *A little later.*

MELINA is putting food and water on the bird-table.

MICHALIS comes on.

He sees MELINA and pauses.

Melina: [*Stops and turns to MICHALIS*] Did it go well?

Michalis: What...?

Melina: The army manoeuvres.

Michalis: Yes.

[*Pause*]

Melina: Why did they come to our island?

Michalis: Why? THAT is why.

Melina: No, I mean why OUR island?

Michalis: No, mother, listen. There is no answer to that. If you like, it's not a real question. They do it.

Melina: And do you know why they do it?

Michalis: No. [*Pause*] I don't know.

[*MICHALIS goes up steps and off*]

[*MELINA looks perplexed*]

[*PADDY comes down steps. He has a bad hangover*]

Paddy: Mrs Petrou...could you please get me some water?

Melina: Of course. You want...?

[*She gestures to suggest a jug*]

Paddy: Yes, please.

[*MELINA goes up steps and off*]

[*SYLVIA comes to top of steps. She is dressed for leaving*]

Sylvia: [*At the point of tears*] I want to go, Paddy.

Paddy: We can't! There's no boat until tomorrow.

Sylvia: I can't stay with the...with the not knowing what's going on! And the...I thought the curfew was supposed to keep the place quiet? You'd be better off without it! What was it last night Paddy?

Paddy: I don't know.

Sylvia: It wasn't right. I know that. I just know.

Paddy: [*Drinks water*] But you don't !

Sylvia: There were soldiers. You told me...and on motorbikes. Up and down. Up and down...

Paddy: Are we back to that? OK. [*Pause*] I've got a book. Do you want me to get it?

Sylvia: What book?

Paddy: It's a book which shows the picture of a festival on an island. Corfu...

Sylvia: Just get me off THIS island Paddy. You were in the navy. You could get us on that boat. Tell them we were on the same side during the war. We were weren't we?

[*Pause*]

[*PADDY wipes his brow feverishly*]

Paddy: Sylvia, this time I'm going to see it through.

Sylvia: See what through?

Paddy: What happened in the war...it could be said I ran away. Well it won't be said again. I'm not going to use THAT navy boat to repeat what happened with the other one. How could you expect...? I won't use that boat to run away.

Sylvia: So you admit it!

Paddy: What?

Sylvia: That there's something to run from!

Paddy: No, I'm not saying that...

Sylvia: You just did!

Paddy: I'm saying we don't know. And if we leave before we DO know, then THAT'S like an act of cowardice. I'll get the book.

[*He goes off up steps*]

Sylvia: [*Shouting after him*] You don't read books Paddy Milanne! You just look at the pictures and decide for yourself what the pictures mean!

[*Silence*]

[*PETROU comes to top of steps. He looks mad though under control*]

[*SYLVIA sits down*]

Petrou: Good morning.

Sylvia: Good morning Mr Petrou. [*Aside*] You don't deserve to wear that uniform.

Petrou: You say...?

[*Silence*]

[*SYLVIA gives PETROU a quick, insincere smile and turns away*]

[*PETROU looks at her back unpleasantly*]

[*MICHALIS comes to top of steps. He carries the 303*]

Petrou: Ah, Michalis!

[*SYLVIA turns to look at PETROU and MICHALIS and then looks back off*]

Petrou: Going shooting?

Michalis: I thought I'd try it out.

Petrou: I could do with a bit of shooting. A hangover always makes me...Did you have any women in Athens?

Michalis: [*After a pause*] No.

[*PETROU wipes his brow*]

[*They come down steps closer to SYLVIA*]

[*PETROU makes an obscene copulating gesture behind SYLVIA's back. He laughs alone*]

[*SYLVIA turns quickly, surprised to find them so close to her*]

[*MICHALIS puts a round in the breech of the rifle*]

[*PADDY comes out again and down steps*]

[*SYLVIA looks momentarily relieved. She looks nervously at MICHALIS from time to time*]

[*PADDY acknowledges PETROU and MICHALIS curtly*]

[*Behind PADDY's back PETROU gives MICHALIS the look of a naughty boy caught in an act. He changes this quickly to an ugly masturbatory mime and a gesture of dismissal*]

[*PADDY takes book to table (Durrell's Greek Islands). He plonks it on the table open*]

Paddy: [*Pointing at photo in book*] Look. The Festival of Saint Spiridion on the island of Corfu. Soldiers, sailors, Church people...

Sylvia: I heard the sound of metal...like chains...

[*MICHALIS pays close attention to SYLVIA*]

Petrou: One thing I can't understand Michalis...

[*MICHALIS makes an urgent motion for his father to be quiet*]

Paddy: You HEARD and you didn't SEE. But anyway, supposing there were chains...

Sylvia: Celebrating a Saint?!

Paddy: But Sylv! [*Short pause*] Saints have had some terrible things done to them, in fact...I remember...in Greek mythology someone WAS chained to a rock. Who knows, Christian festivals sometimes have their roots in Pagan times. And what if they were celebrating Easter? What if they were all carrying crosses? Would that mean they were all going off to be crucified?

Sylvia: They never came back.

Paddy: What?

Sylvia: Why didn't they come back? The boat is still there. They would have to come back to the boat.

[*Pause*]

Petrou: Michalis...

[*SYLVIA and PADDY become attentative to PETROU and MICHALIS*]

Michalis: Did you know that Nana Leros is in there?

Petrou: [*Horrified*] Where?

Michalis: In the hotel.

Petrou: [*Angrily*] You see! [*Pause. Sees the birdtable*] Birds! [*He rushes to birdtable and violently knocks it over*] And the beggar in the hotel. I fucking hate...you know what I fucking hate...? I fucking hate it when women start their fancy business. I know what I can do, I've always known...

[*SYLVIA looks terrified*]

[*PADDY looks perplexed*]

[*PADDY begins to go off*]

[*MICHALIS begins to go off left*]

[*PETROU pauses*]

Petrou: How is it that an operation like this could have allowed these tourists here at the same time?

Michalis: I don't know.

Petrou: It's crazy! Can you see how difficult it makes things for me?

[*He goes off*]

[*MICHALIS goes off*]

Sylvia: [*Upset*] What do you make of all that then Paddy?

Paddy: There's only one way to put our minds at rest. For me to go after that march and find out EXACTLY what it consisted of.

[*PADDY hurries off*]

Sylvia: [*Shouting after him*] Why can't we just go?

[*After a moment there is a great deal of noise off*]

[*PETROU has found NANA and MELINA has become involved*]

[*NANA comes down the steps quickly having been pushed by PETROU*]

[*PETROU comes to the top of the steps followed by MELINA*]

[*SYLVIA looks frightened and confused*]

Melina: Yannis, you're mad!

Nana: [*Tearfully*] I know what's coming.

Petrou: This could build into something too big even for Michalis to handle!

[*NANA stops at bottom of steps. She looks hopefully at MELINA*]

[*MELINA holds PETROU off*]

Melina: Come on Yannis. She's been like this for so long...why do you attack her now...today?

Petrou: They could arrest her but they don't. It's just giving her a free bed. We don't NEED to lock her up now!

Nana: That's true! So ask yourself, Melina, where were they taking those people?

Petrou: [*Raging*] Look at her! What does she do for mankind? Anyone who gets within ten feet of her would never want a woman again!

Nana: They killed the schoolmaster. You know that if they can kill someone who's so respected, they've killed respect itself.

Melina: Stop it Nana.

Petrou: Well you ought to be safe. No one respects you.

[*PETROU gives a forced laugh*]

Nana: Michalis did!

Petrou: [*With threatening gesture*] Then he had no self-respect!

Nana: [*Cowering and stepping back*] The slaves are chaining up the free men!

Melina: [*Complainingly*] Nana!

Petrou: And you're chained to your stink!

Melina: The birdtable!

[*MELINA goes to the birdtable*]

[*SYLVIA gets up to help her*]

Sylvia: I should have done that Mrs Petrou.

Melina: It is alright. Thank you.

Sylvia: Is everything alright?

Melina: Yes.

Petrou: You feed off the scabs of age, Leros, that fall from the people in the street. You're a whore to the dogs. That's why I hate you.

[*MELINA lets out a cry*]

Melina: Yannis!

[*MELINA rushes off up steps*]

[*PETROU pushes NANA off and goes off with her*]

Nana: [*As she goes off*] I know you...

Petrou: [*As he goes off*] For the last time.

[*SYLVIA looks around bewilderedly then goes off the way. PADDY had gone earlier*]

[*There is silence on stage for a moment before lights go down*]

Scene Five

Scene: *A little later.*

SYLVIA is sitting alone.

She flips through the Greek Island book from back to front.

NANA comes on. She slumps onto the steps. She carries a bed-roll.

Nana: You should leave here before it's too late.

Sylvia: It's no good love. I can't understand a word of Greek. [*She looks around sadly*] I don't know what's happening here. I daren't think. Not with Paddy gone so long. I feel so lonely.

Nana: Petrou's been drinking now for two days. He may even turn on you. [*Short pause*] I should have seen what the boy would become. How they'd empty him. How he will do what he must do without working at it. Like a killer who kills in his dreams. That is what a uniform is. I should have KNOWN that his mother wouldn't want to see it. That she will want to think he's still a boy. I should have seen that he would become cruel. Boy or man. His mother will say he's not cruel he's just a boy; his father will say he's not cruel he's a man. I should have seen it all.

[*NANA lays out her blanket on the steps*]

Sylvia: When I hear you speak and see you dressed like that I wonder what went wrong. And now I've seen an island that looked beautiful from the boat, in the sun, suddenly seem to go ugly.

Nana: Shall I tell you about me? When the country was taken over by the gangsters, some refused to join them. Those who did join were cowards. Slaves. Cowards soon turn their guilt to hatred. The good have gone. No one knows where. These people can keep it hidden so that things look normal. Only I, who only ever wanted communion, have been left without a friend. I was a fool. You can't have communion without society. So there's nowhere to go but here. I make my bed. Or my coffin. [*Short pause*] What happens now? Now that life's no longer normal? Now that they've made the island a dungeon? Now that there's no longer any attempt to hide? They'll get bolder.

Sylvia: You sound as lonely as I feel love. I feel I know what you're saying. But what difference does it make? I couldn't help you even if I did know.

[*MELINA comes on, unseen by the others, to the top of the steps*]

Sylvia: I think you need to get off this island.

[*MICHALIS comes on behind SYLVIA carrying a small, dead dog*]

[*NANA has her head hung down*]

[*MICHALIS throws the dog onto the steps near NANA*]

[*NANA shrieks*]

[*MELINA gasps with shock and goes off*]

[*SYLVIA gasps*]

[*NANA looks at dog*]

Nana: It's the schoolmaster's! Did you kill it?

Michalis: Of course.

Nana: But you loved this dog!

Michalis: My father is having some difficulty with you. You should know: a son will do anything to please his father. I need to come up to his expectation.

Nana: I know why you killed this man's dog. To try and kill the memory of what they've done to him. Michalis, he tried to save you! He tried to teach you...don't you know that? Don't you?

[*Silence*]

Nana: Do you know that he tried to stop your father beating you?

[*MICHALIS hits NANA angrily*]

[*For a moment they pause with the horror of the realisation that this is the first time that he's hit her*]

[*NANA lets out a cry and rushes off*]

[*MICHALIS picks up NANA's blanket using the barrel of his gun and throws it after her. He kicks the dog away*]

[*He suddenly begins pacing up and down the steps*]

[*MELINA comes to the top of the steps*]

[*MICHALIS stops*]

[*SYLVIA uses the opportunity to go*]

[*MELINA pauses as if not knowing what to say to MICHALIS*]

[*MICHALIS sits on steps where NANA sat*]

Melina: The last time I was in Athens, Michalis, not long ago, I came to a small street near Constitution Square. I saw a crowd so I went up to it. As I got close, someone threw a bucket of human waste from a window high up on the other side of the street. The crowd rushed apart. Some people were laughing. As I came closer I could see that on the pavement there was a man with no legs sitting on a piece of cardboard. The stuff had hit him. He was soaking wet. He stank. He had two crutches and was thrashing about with them. [*Pause*] Then a young man came up to him and there seemed to be a moment when everything froze. The young man suddenly hit the beggar on the back of the neck. At that moment the people seemed...freed...to do what they wanted. They began hitting and kicking the beggar. I left because I thought I could hear the sound of his flesh collapsing.

[*MELINA goes to the dead dog. She picks it up by the tail and goes off with it*]

[*PADDY comes on carrying the broken off bottom-half of an oar. He is drunk*]

Paddy: [*With humour*] Water!

[*MICHALIS turns to him*]

[*PADDY takes some water. He drinks and gasps. He makes a gesture putting his hand to his forehead to indicate that he's drunk too much*]

Paddy: Ouzo! [*Pause. Holding up oar*]. The very oar that Ulysses used to get back to his wife!

[*PADDY laughs*]

Paddy: No point in talking to you son. I can see that. Greek.

Michalis: You must be careful how much you drink.

Paddy: [*Shocked*] Christ! He speaks English! [*Pause*] I wonder if I've said anything.

Michalis: Where have you been?

Paddy: [*Sitting*] I've been to Homer's little Cave. I had to. [*Short pause*] My wife's paranoid...where is she?

[*Silence*]

Paddy: She'll be back! She's a neurotic. [*He holds his hands in front of him shaking them*] Nerves. It can get to you...when it comes to mystery and adventure, she lives in the dark ages. [*Holds up oar*] For me...let me tell you: we're all sailors.

[*PADDY drinks more water*]

Paddy: It's once in a blue moon! Holiday! Greece! Me and Greece go back a long way. You won't remember this but you may know; somewhere, amongst one of these islands, in the war, a boat... [*Pause. Suddenly tight with tears.*]...was blown up.

[*Silence*]

Paddy: [*Regaining self-control*] In the war. The Second World War. Don't you know?

[*MELINA comes on. She looks desperately sad and preoccupied*]

[*She comes to NANA's blanket and folds it carefully. She puts it on the steps*]

[*PADDY pauses and watches her for a moment*]

[*MICHALIS looks at her bemused*]

[*When she finishes she goes off up steps*]

Paddy: We were in this region. The Balkans. We fought for you. And another thing - we were on your side. In the civil war. Did you know that? [*Pause*] You know about the civil war?

Michalis: No...I don't know.

Paddy: It doesn't matter. It was won. [*Sadly*] Looking down there at that sea where that boat might have sunk...seeing you come home, the returning hero, reminded me...my old man - my Father was a street man; he had his faults - we all have - but he believed in tradition. If you like, in a sense, that's what the curfew's for. To protect history and tradition. If you protect history and tradition then you know that history and tradition will protect you. One thing I think my wife forgot to remember - we're not home, we're in Greece. [*Short pause*] Anyway, my old man, when I got home he kicked shit out of me. I don't care. I had it coming. It was no way to behave. It showed a lack of respect...

[*MELINA comes out with a wiping cloth and table cloth(s). She wipes tables silently and puts on table cloth(s)*]

[*PADDY pauses and watches her*]

Michalis: Mama, what are you doing?

Melina: [*A little distractedly*] It is my home isn't it Michalis? This island is my home?

Michalis: Yes, but...

Paddy: I was just telling your son about history and tradition. You tend to forget. But today, I've seen quiet ancient lanes where who knows who walked down years ago. Great men in great days.

Petrou: [*From inside hotel with affected, tragic tone*] Michalis!

[*MICHALIS looks up at hotel*]

Melina: He's still drunk.

[*She finishes with the table cloths and hurries off up steps*]

Michalis: [*After her*] Mama!

[*MICHALIS goes off after his mother*]

[*PADDY begins to sing a sea-shanty*]

[*After a moment, SYLVIA goes on*]

Sylvia: Paddy! I'm glad you're back.

Paddy: Sylv! I was wondering where you'd got to.

[*He breathes deep, happily*]

Paddy: What a day!

Sylvia: [*Slumping into a chair*] You look as if you've been drinking.

Paddy: I had a couple. It's thirsty weather.

Sylvia: What did you see Paddy?

Paddy: What did I see when?

Sylvia: The whatever it was in the night!

Paddy: To tell you the truth, Sylv, I gave it a miss. What was the point?

[*SYLVIA starts angrily*]

Paddy: Cool down now Sylv! The thing is...I'm more and more convinced that this was the place. The place where the boat went down.

Sylvia: God!

Paddy: And look. [*He holds up the oar*] Ulysses' oar, I'm calling it. [*Gives a little laugh*] But there is a connection.

Sylvia: Paddy, you make me sick.

Paddy: Christ Sylv! Don't...you're not getting into the spirit are you? We ARE on a Greek island that Ulysses or someone like him could well have landed on. I was a sailor; HE was a sailor. This is a once in a lifetime chance to feel that...to look out at that "wine-dark" sea.

Sylvia: [*Scoffingly*] Listen to this! Paddy the poet!

Paddy: You've got to see how it is! [*Pause. Maudlin*] It's my history. Lying out there in that bay - my agony...[*Pause. Controlling*] And what if the worst of your fears were true and they were prisoners? Though, I've got to say it, since last night I, at least, have hardly seen a soldier.

[*SYLVIA makes a noise of exasperation and turns her head*]

Paddy: Well it's true! Haven't things quietened down? Listen! [*Pause*] You can hardly hear a thing. Supposing you're right. At least we can go home and we can say WE saw it.

Sylvia: [*Angrily*] What's the point in seeing it?

Paddy: The point is...to put it crudely Sylv, we're on holiday! We're sight SEErs!

Sylvia: Well let me tell you about a sight I saw! That soldier, that son, came from god only knows where, carrying a dead dog which I suppose he'd shot because he went off with a rifle WHICH he loaded here, and he threw the dead dog at that tramp woman who was sitting over there on those steps.

[*Silence*]

Paddy: [*Incredulously*] A soldier throwing dead dogs around? [*Pause*] Did he speak to her as he gave her the dog?

Sylvia: He didn't GIVE her the dog! He THREW it at her! And what difference does it make if he DID speak? I wouldn't 've understood.

Paddy: Well what I was trying to get at was whether he shouted his head off or whether he spoke reasonably.

Sylvia: He didn't shout, no.

Paddy: So he could have been saying quite quietly: "Here you are, I've brought you a dead dog to eat".

Sylvia: Nobody brings anybody a dead dog to eat!

Paddy: How do YOU know? They view dogs differently here. In different parts of the world they have different habits. And don't forget: she's a tramp. Tramps will eat anything. They live in another world. They live in the world of the carrion crow and the rat. You ask the landlady if this woman has ever eaten a dog before.

Sylvia: The dog was left here! The tramp didn't take it off to eat it or anything!

[*Silence*]

Sylvia: The whole thing was full of violence. Paddy, I think...

Paddy: Let me tell you what I just saw. I went into a restaurant to get a little drink...

Sylvia: You mean a pub!

Paddy: They don't have pubs here! [*Holds his arms out*] See...? If you mean a bar, alright, I went into this bar for a drink. Do you know what I saw?

[*MELINA comes down steps. She carries a brush*]

Paddy: A man with no nose. No nose at all.

[*MELINA begins sweeping up*]

Paddy: The landlady might know him. [*To MELINA, holding his hand to his face to indicate a nose*] A man with no nose. You know him?

Melina: [*Preoccupied*] Yes I know him. He's a policeman.

Paddy: [*Surprised*] A policeman with no nose! A sight like that, that's violence. It was like having a drink with a cyclops. I nearly filled my pants...

Sylvia: Paddy! I'm telling you. I know that woman is in danger!

Paddy: What woman?

Sylvia: [*In an undertone to PADDY as* MELINA *gets nearer*] The tramp!

Paddy: How do you know that?

Sylvia: I was sitting here with her wasn't I?

Paddy: Well what were you doing? What were you doing to let you know...

Sylvia: We were talking.

Paddy: Who was talking?

Sylvia: Me and the tramp woman!

Paddy: But you don't speak the same language!

Sylvia: So what Paddy! We're not speaking the same language are we? I'm telling you, you've got to help that woman. Use your influence. Go down to that boat...

Paddy: Don't start that again!

Sylvia: Go down to that boat and use your influence to get that woman off this island.

Paddy: We've been over it Sylvia. I've explained...

Sylvia: You haven't explained...

Paddy: I told you...

Sylvia: I thought you were a socialist. Well if you're a socialist Paddy Milanne, people may as well give up sharing!

Paddy: [*Mockingly*] Christ, Sylv, you don't know what you're talking about! Get me a drink...

[*MELINA goes off up steps*]

Sylvia: [*Also mockingly*] Socialist!

Paddy: I'm a democrat first and foremost. That's what I am. That's why I listen to you!

Sylvia: If you're a democrat you may as well give the vote to dogs!

Paddy: [*Getting up angrily*] You're getting offens...

Sylvia: I don't see how you can be a democrat if you can't face the truth!

Paddy: Truth!

Sylvia: Yes, truth! The reason you won't go down to that boat is because you're afraid of them! You're afraid they might think you ARE a democrat...

Paddy: [*Stung*] Afraid!

[*MELINA comes out with a bucket of whitewash which she puts at the bottom of the steps*]

Sylvia: Especially that they might think you're a socialist helping an old woman...

[*MELINA goes off up steps*]

Paddy: The sun's got to you!

[*PADDY goes off up steps*]

Sylvia: [*Shouting after him*] Coward!

[*After a moment, MELINA comes down steps with a bucket of water and cloth. She puts the bucket down near the whitewash and begins washing the steps*]

[*SYLVIA sees her and goes to her*]

Sylvia: [*Seeing whitewash*] It looks like you're preparing for a big job.

[*MELINA stops washing but doesn't get up*]

Melina: It is difficult to tell that it's a home anymore. The steps are almost black; the walls...as if it was a...hall for the army.

[*MELINA washes steps again*]

[*MICHALIS comes to top of steps*]

Michalis: Mama, stop it!

Melina: [*Sharply*] Why?

[*MELINA pauses*]

[*MICHALIS is silent*]

Melina: Tell me Michalis.

[*Silence*]

Melina: When I was pregnant with you I wanted to leave this island.

[*MICHALIS looks uncomfortable*]

[*SYLVIA doesn't understand. She turns and goes to sit down. She takes water to the birdtable instead*]

Melina: To me, this was no place to bring up a child. There's too much ignorance...

Michalis: [*Seeing SYLVIA with the water*] Look Mama! Why doesn't she leave it alone? We've been too polite with these tourists.

Melina: ...here. [*Pause*] In spite of the school. I knew it would be difficult to teach you.

Michalis: [*About SYLVIA*] As far as she knows we don't want it touched. What's it go to do with her? Excuse me!

[*SYLVIA turns to him*]

Michalis: Please, do not. We will be moving it so there is no point.

Sylvia: Oh, I'm sorry.

[*SYLVIA looks a little hurt. She sits*]

Melina: Your father wouldn't leave here. He never had the courage to leave. You have to have courage to make decisions like that.

[*SYLVIA, obviously uncomfortable, gets up. She looks off*]

[*MICHALIS pays most attention to her*]

Melina: We stayed. I hid from the truth. The truth was not that I wanted to leave and didn't; the truth was that, to save the family, to keep it secure, I let your father force me into accepting what he wanted. It's been like that ever since. It cost me a lot to make this home.

[*She washes the steps*]

Michalis: But Mama, things are different now. This is what I was trying to say. There are more important ways of looking at things than from the point of view of the family. Now, those who follow Colonel Papadopoulos are the courageous. And he is our teacher.

Melina: [*Shouting angrily*] What does Mr Papadopoulos teach you apart from how to kill dogs?

[*SYLVIA looks upset and goes up steps*]

[*Silence*]

Melina: How could you do it Michalis? THAT is what I don't understand. How could you do that? If I could understand that then maybe I could understand what else has happened here. I don't know...just in the space of a day it feels that my whole world's been changed. But maybe not...maybe it's been longer. Tell me how you could have done it Michalis.

Michalis: Mama! Does it matter? Does anybody in Greece care about dogs?

Melina: You did!

Michalis: [*Coming down steps*] But Mama, if you only knew...it's as if...I don't know...to believe in this hero! On the day we finished in the barracks, they said: "tomorrow you will meet the leader".

[*He sits*]

Michalis: "Sleep well tonight", they said. Then the siren sounded. Anyone not in bed would be beaten.

[*MELINA looks hurt*]

[*MICHALIS seems almost distracted*]

Michalis: That way they ensure that when the men later patrol the streets of our cities and towns or even OUR streets, they know how to deal with those who break the curfew. I see how important it is to defend the Colonel's curfew. I belong to a patrol that exists all over Greece.

[*The sound of PADDY and SYLVIA arguing can be heard*]

[*The only words that should be heard are, from PADDY: "Ulysses" and from SYLVIA, "excuses" and "open your eyes"*]

Melina: Are you trying to say that Nana breaks the curfew when she is forced to live out in the night?

[*Bouzouki music begins in the hotel*]

Michalis: The next day they lined us up. We waited at attention for about an hour. The door opened. We were allowed to watch as the Colonel entered. The genius. He is not a very big man. He stood before us and, Mama, this is what he said: "For you men the emotional life is over. From now on you lead the intellectual life. The life of winning the argument".

[*PETROU lets out a cry of happiness from off*]

Melina: I don't know what this genius has done.

[*PETROU comes on, half-drunk, carrying a tray with a jug of rezina, a bottle of ouzo and some glasses. He almost dances to the music*]

[*MELINA sees him and turns away horrified*]

Petrou: Melina, you'd better go and do something about that woman. I think she's beating up her husband! [*He laughs*].

[*MELINA gets up. She rushes off up steps*]

Melina: [*As she goes*] Did you know that your son killed a dog?

[*She goes off*]

[*From this point the lighting should begin to dim so that by the end of the scene it's quite dark*]

[*PETROU puts tray on table*]

Petrou: [*Happily surprised*] YOU killed a dog?

[*MICHALIS goes to table*]

[*PETROU pours drinks*]

Michalis: I wanted to warn Nana Leros.

Petrou: That bitch! I should have known she'd have something to do with it. [*Pause*] I notice there's been a marked change in you since you went away, Michalis. You've grown up.

[*PADDY suddenly appears at the top of the steps. He is shouting back into hotel*]

[*PETROU and MICHALIS look at him with surprise*]

Paddy: Look, as far as I'm concerned, there's NOTHING more important than a man getting his holiday. And I speak as a trade union official Sylvia. You don't know what work is until you know your holiday. Only most men don't know what their holiday is. They think it's for SLEEP. Well I'm here to show them...if there's nothing else I can do in my life...that holidays are for...well, seeing things you wouldn't normally see!

[*Silence*]

Sylvia: [*From off*] Paddy!

[*PADDY goes back in*]

[*PETROU and MICHALIS look at each other*]

Petrou: What happened to the dog?

Michalis: I don't know.

[*PETROU gives MICHALIS a glass. They both drink. PETROU gulps. MICHALIS sips*]

Petrou: She probably took it away to eat. She's got no fucking morality. She gets the thing killed and goes off and eats it! There's something wrong with a world that can give birth to a bitch like that.

Michalis: [*After a pause*] I hit her. I think it was only at that moment that I fully understood my training.

Petrou: You hit her too! [*Pause*] I salute you Michalis.

[*PETROU drinks*]

Michalis: [*A little distractedly*] Number One cell in the security building on Bouboulinas Street faces onto Tosita Street.

[*PETROU gives MICHALIS a puzzled look*]

Michalis: There's a new maternity hospital on Tosita Street. From Number One cell you can hear the cries of the communists being punished on the terrace. The cries of the communists would be confused with the cries of the women giving birth in the hospital. It was difficult to know which was which. Some nights when you were very confused you thought the women were communists. I began to think that every woman in the hospital was one; that they were giving birth to lepers and parasites. I hated them. It was as if there was a factory just across the road turning out the enemy. I was right. One day a young woman sat up in bed and gave me a big wave. I thought: she's one. She thinks I'm one too, that's why she's waving. I took my head away from the window in disgust. A minute or two later I looked out again. Now there's a family round the bed. They're all waving and holding up the little communist baby.

[*PETROU looks confused*]

Petrou: Why were YOU in that cell?

Michalis: They were training me. They'd leave me in a cell for whole days and nights, naked, with a white light that never went out. Sometimes the door would burst open and three or four soldiers would rush in and beat me up. Then they'd leave me alone again.

Petrou: It doesn't make sense! Why did they beat YOU up?

Michalis: I told you. It was training. When it came to be my turn to rush into a cell and kick and punch someone, I'd do it more whole-heartedly. Only when I did it, it would be to a communist.

Petrou: These tactics are new to me. [*He drinks*] To be beaten up to make you go and beat up someone else! That's a stroke of genius!

[*MICHALIS drinks*]

[*PETROU fills the glasses*]

Michalis: When they first did it, it was a shock. Like someone jumping out at you in a dark alley. You just feel the pain. When they picked us up at the Pireus they took us to the barracks. As we jumped out of the truck they beat us on the head with clubs. They beat us in the yard for about ten minutes then they took us inside and beat us for another ten minutes. Then they locked us away and beat us individually. [*He begins to laugh madly and* *uncontrollably*] They gave us food, we had drill then they beat us again. After a few days we'd beat each other up! One would be singled out and attacked in the yard. The next day he'd be in the group beating him up the day before! We got used to it so we knew what to expect.

[*PETROU looks preoccupied. He is laughing a little but with his mind on something else*]

[*MICHALIS's laughter subsides suddenly*]

[*MELINA comes to the top of steps but isn't seen by the other two*]

Petrou: One thing you don't know Michalis. I killed someone. In the civil war. Nothing close-quarters like you. I didn't have the satisfaction of being near to the bastard as he died. But I saw him fall. I was cheered. I tell you, I felt fucking god-like. I almost cried tears of pure joy as my bullet felled the fucker.

[*MELINA's horror grows as she listens*]

Michalis: If they caught you crying they'd beat you up even harder. I cried. After the first day I cried all night.

[*MELINA turns away but remains where she is*]

Michalis: I thought they were going to kill me. But you soon learn you're not going to die. The only thing you have to tackle then is the pain. It's impossible to live with the pain so you deaden yourself to it. One of the greatest weapons against the communists is that they don't know if they're going to die or not. But you know how far to take them without killing them because you've been through it. In fact, when you jump in on them and start beating them with the iron bar, they wish they were going to die.

Petrou: [*Intrigued*] You beat them with an iron bar? What did that feel like?

Michalis: [*Emptily*] Like hitting meat.

Petrou: [*After a thoughtful pause*] You've done more in three months than I've done all my life.

[*Pause. They both drink deep*]

Michalis: One recruit didn't make it.

Petrou: What do you mean he didn't make it?

Michalis: He refused to take part in it.

Petrou: You mean he was a coward?

Michalis: I don't know. They beat him up more than they beat up anyone else. He just wouldn't do it back.

Petrou: I wish I'd been there. I'd've made him do it.

Michalis: You're right in a way. If you'd been there all his life. I thought: "I could never be like that boy because of my father".

Petrou: That's right! You're a Petrou. Now you can see that I was good for you.

Melina: You were wrong Yannis. The past is never dead. It's just that we think it is. When we think there's a change it's just the past coming to life. All that we've hidden stands discovered before us. Michalis, why have you plotted against me?

Michalis: I haven't Mama.

Melina: But you've turned my island into a prison!

Michalis: I wanted to protect you. I didn't want to tell you...

Melina: Protect me from what?

Michalis: I didn't want you to worry.

Melina: Worry! Worry about what? That there are desperate people here who might escape and kill me? But don't you think I'd find out about them? Don't you think I'd worry then? ...[*Pause*] Unless...unless...we are to leave? Is that it son? We have to leave?

[*Silence*]

Petrou: You're getting on my nerves, Melina! Go to bed!

Michalis: It's true we have to leave. [*Suddenly angrily*] Yes it's true we have to leave! We have to make this small sacrifice. Or would you rather we become helots to the Russians. Rather we were overrun by communists?

Melina: But they are here! On my island! In my home! How is THAT protecting me?

[*She runs off crying*]

Petrou: Christ!

[*They both drink*]

Michalis: There was one thing...

Petrou: Yes, go on son.

Michalis: It's difficult to describe. [*Short pause*] Beating up a communist gave you a feeling of comradeship. It was the loneliness. [*Pause*] When they left you alone and beat you every few hours, you felt like a stranger in the world. You felt the whole world hated you. You didn't know why they were doing this to you. You felt as lonely as if they'd tied you to a cold mountainside and left you for the frost. When they let you beat a communist you got a strong feeling of belonging that made you want to work harder at the beating. [*Pause*] All except for that boy. He hanged himself. They kept him isolated more than anyone else.

Petrou: Don't start feeling sorry for the bastard.

Michalis: I'm not feeling sorry for him. I don't feel sorry anymore. I couldn't understand it, that's all. It didn't make sense. The system should have been watertight.

Petrou: A bit like these tourists turning up with the army! Christ!

[*They drink*]

Petrou: That kid must have been a communist. That's why he wouldn't beat up the other communists! You should have seen that straight away!

Michalis: Maybe.

Petrou: Every ordinary human being would have done what every other ordinary human being was doing. [*Pause*] I look forward to the day when I can have a bash at a communist again. Most of the opportunities on this island have been used up. They all support the government. You can't even touch Nana Leros on that score. She's a tramp. Everyone knows that tramps are not communists. Even though she's always on about communion. So why doesn't she go to fucking church?

Michalis: What do you mean?

Petrou: She's always saying she wants communion but you tell her to go to church and she says she doesn't mean that. She says she's looking for something else.

Michalis: Yes, she is.

Petrou: What?

Michalis: Socialism.

[*PETROU looks stunned*]

Petrou: Christ!

[*He drains his glass*]

Petrou: Now I come to think of it, she accused Colonel Papadopoulos of stealing her money. Isn't that proof?

Michalis: I remember one man who was brought in. He said those very words: "Papadopoulos stole my money". Then he spat at me.

Petrou: [*Indignant*] What, no colonel or mister, just fucking Papadopoulos and then he spat? What for?

Michalis: He was being defiant.

Petrou: He wouldn't've been defiant if I'd been there! I'd've broken every bastard bone in his body!

[*PETROU drinks down*]

Michalis: Wait a minute Papa! I want to tell you what we did with him.

[*PETROU fills his glass and tops up MICHALIS's*]

Michalis: The first thing: we stripped him. Like all communists he had dirty pants...

Petrou: [*With disgust*] What do you mean? Shit?

Michalis: Yes.

Petrou: Christ!

Michalis: It made us angry too. We tied his hands and feet and hung him by the wrists. Then we spun him round. Everyone could give him a good whack wherever they wanted to.

Petrou: Mostly round the bottom part of his body I suppose.

Michalis: What do you mean?

Petrou: Well if you've got him hung up you're not going to be dealing with the head.

Michalis: The head came later. As we watched him spin and heard his screams we were all thinking: "We've had this done to us. And we didn't do anything wrong! So why should we have any pity on this man?"

[*PETROU drinks in agreement*]

Michalis: We cut him down so that he fell and cracked his skull. We got a bench and put it in the centre of the room and got the communist and tied him to it.

[*PETROU is almost rubbing his hands with anticipation*]

Michalis: Then we gagged him with a rag that was soaked in our piss.

Petrou: [*Joyfully*] Whose idea was that?

Michalis: I don't know. I think it's always been done. In the end we got a bucket which we kept full with piss. We'd just keep the rags in there soaking. [*Pause*] Where was I Papa?

Petrou: You said you had him on the bench and you gagged him with this piss rag.

Michalis: Then we hit him on the bottom of the feet.

Petrou: [*With incredulity*] On the bottom of the feet?

Michalis: You don't understand Papa. There's nothing more painful. Sometimes we keep the shoes on and hit with a lead pipe. That's even worse. They say it makes the brain bounce around in the head. And it makes the feet swell up like balloons. When you've had that for four hours you know all about it. After that, we untie

him, stand him up and make him run around the bench. He can
hardly stand let alone run so we have to give him a bit of
encouragement. We beat him all over the body.

[*PETROU splutters into his drink laughing at MICHALIS's last line*]

Petrou: Is that it?

Michalis: In this case it was. He was bleeding so badly that the
doctor told us to stop.

Petrou: [*Laughing*] I'm glad of that Michalis. I thought for a moment
you were going to tell me you let the bastard get away with it.

Michalis: They wrapped him in a blanket and took him off to
solitary. Just as they were dragging him out, I managed to ask:
"Who stole your money"? He didn't want to say anything then.

[*MELINA comes to the top of the steps again. She has been crying. She
looks distracted*]

Melina: What can I do? You were right, Yannis. This is a change
there's no going back on. And Nana, she was right...

Petrou: Fucking Nana...

Melina: I've been your slave Yannis...

Petrou: [*About MELINA*] What's she raving about Michalis?

Melina: ...because I let you dominate me. In my family. And that's
why I've let Papadopoulos dominate me. You have to fight them
to remain free but if you fight them they chain you up. But what
can slaves do with free men? They can't use them. This is such a
terrible thing. Tell me it's not true Michalis. They're going to kill
them aren't they? I believe they're over on our beach now waiting
to be shot. Don't you understand? This is like the end of the
world! They're murdering people in my living room! And
Papadopoulos told us this is what he was saving us from!

[*MELINA lets out a cry*]

Michalis: [*Calmly*] Colonel Papadopoulos has said: "Greek justice is
and always will be the best justice that ever existed in human
society." You'll see that on the walls in Athena. And on the streets
you'll see calm. Our island has been chosen as the place of
tribunal. That's what you don't understand Mama. When we get to
Athena you'll be better. You'll see, you'll be happy there.

[*MELINA lets out another cry and rushes off*]

Petrou: It'll be something just to get her away from that tramp.

Michalis: If Nana lived in Athena, she'd be in Bouboulinas Street. On
the terrace.

Petrou: She wouldn't and you know it! She'd be fucking dead! They'd have every right to knock her off by way of repayment for all the charity she's taken.

[*Pause*]

Petrou: [*Leaning across the table towards MICHALIS*] Let's face it Michalis. You've proved something haven't you? You've proved that communists are dangerous. [*Pause*] By having to take that kind of action against them! You wouldn't have to beat up somebody who wasn't dangerous would you?

[*Silence*]

Petrou: Let's go for a drink. Homer's cave.

[*They go off*]

[*Lights down*]

Scene Six

Scene: *Night. Before the curfew.*

SYLVIA is sitting on the steps with NANA.

Sylvia: I feel much better now. Now I know we're going tomorrow. I've got Paddy tucked up nicely in bed sleeping it off; I've packed my things. All I have to do is have a little wash. It'll be hot tonight. Paddy'll be sweating. He always does after a drink. Even in winter. I'll have to get a few things in Athens. Then off to the airport. I'll be glad to get home really. When I'm home having my cup of tea with Rhona this will all seem like a film. And Paddy'll be off down the Legion causing controversy like he always does when he returns home. That's what gives him his pull: he becomes the centre of attention. He never takes things very seriously. You don't have to if you've got the gift of the gab like Pad. The only time he takes things seriously is if they happen to him by accident. Then it's someone else who makes him see the seriousness of it. Mind you, he always manages to wheedle his way out and make it all sound like good sense from the political point of view. But then, in the end, where we live, it doesn't make much difference does it? After Paddy's done his party piece, everything's the same no matter what side you're on. I dare say with the most of them you could drive a tank up their street and the only thing they'd feel is a bit jealous.

[*PADDY comes to top of steps. He is drunk though not in any stumbling sense. He breathes deep*]

Paddy: By Christ! I'm breathing air that hasn't changed for centuries. This IS paradise.

Sylvia: [*Turning, shocked*] Paddy, why aren't you in bed!

Paddy: Bed is for the sick and the tired.

Sylvia: Well I should be there then because I'm sick and tired of you. [*Indicating table*] Just sit down there Paddy and be quiet.

Paddy: [*Light-heartedly*] Sylv! It's our last night! You don't expect me to...

Sylvia: You're not going off drinking again? For god's sake Paddy, you want to grow up!

Paddy: [*Giving SYLVIA a peck on the cheek*] I am. That's why I'm only going to have one.

[*PADDY goes down steps*]

Sylvia: You make sure you get back here soon. You've always got to spoil everything. I was just starting to relax.

[*PADDY goes off*]

Sylvia: Homer's bloody cave!

[*MELINA comes to top of steps. She looks weak and depressed*]

Melina: Nana.

[*NANA and SYLVIA look at MELINA*]

Nana: Melina! [*She gets up*] What?...

[*MELINA comes close to NANA. MELINA suddenly begins crying. NANA puts her arms around her*]

[*SYLVIA looks distressed. While MELINA speaks, SYLVIA gets up with a look that suggests she just doesn't want to witness any more agony. She does to the bottom of the steps, moves around the front and eventually goes up steps into hotel*]

Melina: [*Through her tears*] Nana, I don't...I don't under...I don't understand...what's happened to...to people? People who give birth to babies and feed them and...clothes...people who grow the food, make the clothes...socks, coats...people who look after the babies, the children...send them to hospital if they're sick...nurses, people who drive the ambulances; people who build the roads to drive the ambulances on. Police to keep the roads safe for the ambulances...people using radios, people who MADE the radio people who invented telephones, people who keep the telephones working people in newspapers people on television people who can show the way the TRUTH people in robes and ceremonies people on thrones churches palaces people in courts in glasses wigs people with KNOWLEDGE intelligence in schools teaching children...

[*She suddenly stops*]

[*NANA hugs her tightly*]

[*Lights down*]

Scene Seven

Scene: *Night. Siren sounds during blackout.*

NANA is sleeping on the steps with her blanket around her.

We can hear PADDY singing off,the Cahn/Van Heusen song "It's nice to go trav'ling". There are others trying to hum along with him without much success.

NANA raises her head. She gasps and pulls the blanket right over her curling up on steps.

PADDY comes on with PETROU and MICHALIS on either side of him.

PETROU sees NANA on steps and stops singing.

MICHALIS also stops singing.

PADDY's singing dies away.

PETROU goes quickly to NANA. He leaves PADDY having a little difficulty with standing.

PETROU leaves NANA and comes to PADDY and MICHALIS. He puts his arms around them so that they form a conspiratorial group facing the audience.

Petrou: The way she's laying, I could do her in with just one thrust of my foot.

[*PADDY looks bemused*]

Paddy: [*With a laugh*] I don't speak Greek!

[*PETROU laughs*]

Petrou: [*Quietly to PADDY*] Shall I do it?

[*PADDY shrugs*]

Petrou: [*Nodding affirmatively as he speaks*] Just tell me I should.

[*PADDY nods affirmatively but he's bemused*]

[*PETROU looks at MICHALIS and laughs*]

[*PETROU goes to NANA quickly and quietly*]

[*PADDY finds a chair and slumps in it with his back to PETROU*]

[*PETROU deftly puts his foot to NANA's neck and presses quickly and powerfully*]

[*NANA lets out a cry and dies*]

[*Silence*]

[*MICHALIS looks impassive*]

[*PETROU comes to PADDY*]

Petrou: [*Indicating NANA*] Want a fuck? Now's your chance.

Paddy: [*Bemused*] You mean what do I think? I think you should put her where she belongs.

[*PETROU looks at MICHALIS and grins*]

Petrou: You could do us a favour. You could find out if she's dead or alive. The only way you can find out if a woman is dead or alive is to fuck her.

[*PETROU laughs*]

[*PADDY laughs without knowing why*]

Petrou: You have to be certain. And it's hard to be certain even about certainties! I mean everybody thought it was a certainty that you'd never get a military government in Greece - the mother and father of fucking democracies!

[*PETROU laughs*]

[*PADDY laughs with difficulty: he wants to sleep*]

[*PETROU goes to MICHALIS*]

[*PADDY falls asleep*]

[*PETROU points to PADDY and laughs*]

[*PETROU puts an arm around MICHALIS and they go off up steps*]

[*After a moment or two, MELINA comes on down steps. She goes to NANA and looks at her closely. She gasps*]

[*SYLVIA comes to top of steps and begins to come down them tentatively*]

Melina: She's dead.

Sylvia: What? I don't know what you're saying.

[*MELINA turns to SYLVIA*]

Melina: She is dead. They have killed her.

[*SYLVIA is shocked*]

Sylvia: [*With difficulty*] Who?

Melina: These men.

[*Silence in which SYLVIA's world is collapsing*]

Sylvia: What can we do?

Melina: What can I do? I have the army in my living room.

[*MELINA gets up. She goes off distractedly*]

[SYLVIA slumps onto steps looking at PADDY with incredulity]
[Lights down]

Scene Eight

Scene: *Later. Lighter. Nearer morning.*

PADDY is still sleeping in chair.

On a tape played loudly in the auditorium, we hear SYLVIA's voice. She is on the telephone. She is tearful.

A dog barks throughout.

Sylvia: If I could speak Greek this would be hard but I can't which makes it all the more hard. *[Short pause]* I want to get the army, the NAVY...I don't know - WAR out of my living room. She said it. She said it and she's gone. Run away. I can't run away can I? He's MY husband. *[Pause]* I want...I want the police. *[Pause]* HELLO! *[Pause]* The police!...*[Pause]* I told you: I DON'T SPEAK GREEK! *[Spelling the words out]* Po..lice. And Am...bu...lance. Po...God! God, god, god! *[Pause. Tears]* Well what about embassy? EMB... ASSY? AM...BASS...ADOR? Athens! For god's...*[Pause]* Athens, yes, yes, yes. *[Pause]* What? *[Suddenly beside herself]* Can't you get somebody who speaks English! Can't you get someone civilised! God! Ambulance! POLICE! *[She mimics the sound of a siren]* Na, na, na, na, na, na, na, na...

[The sound of her doing this gets louder before suddenly stopping]
[Lights down]

END

what it is about you Lomax but you're not a conscientious objector. [*Pause*] You're too English.

Lomax: I was born in Ashby de la Zouche! [*Pause*]. What does it mean, Colonel, to be English? I used to go camping before the war, near the sea. Why do people like the sea? Because the sea belongs to itself? Because it's free? I remember one morning waking to a lot of noise. Children playing. A dog barking and a man shouting. One man said to another man with anger: "I'm going to get my tent up quickly before your dog gets a chance to shit again on my ground!".

[*LOMAX laughs*]

[*He begins to go*]

Dangerfield: Wait, Lomax. Don't go. [*DANGERFIELD waves BRAUN to him with his hand*] Please!

[*BRAUN comes on breathless*]

[*BRAUN looks at LOMAX with hatred*]

Dangerfield: Your Germans work well. Some water?

Braun: [*Accent*] Water? Yes. The sun! Phew!

[*LOMAX goes a little way from the desk and lays down. He props himself on one elbow and chews a sprig of grass*]

[*DANGERFIELD pours Braun some water*]

[*BRAUN drinks greedily*]

Braun: My Germans work better than the Italians. But they are so thirsty! They are dying of thirst! The Italians are used to the sun but they have no belly for IT! They have figs for balls!

[*DANGERFIELD fills BRAUN's glass again*]

Dangerfield: Do you know what it is to be English?

[*BRAUN drinks greedily. When he finishes he looks blankly at DANGERFIELD*]

[*Silence*]

Dangerfield: The soil, the land of England, has such an unremitting pull that in it we seek to immerse our identity. Our individualism is even subordinate to the great humanitarian pull of the land.

[*LOMAX makes a scoffing noise*]

Dangerfield: Its humanitarianism is its hunger for the English human. That's why these barren skies are such a tragedy. The land needs to prosper if England is to prosper. We need rain.

[BRAUN looks preoccupied and hopeful]

Dangerfield: Without rain,the sun evaporates the water and a little bit of England goes up to the sky.

[LOMAX lays down fully with a groan]

Braun: *[Feverishly]* It is the same with German! The German has put his head in the mind...the conscience of Hitler. This is it. I know this! I am a conscientious supporter of war. Do you know why? Because my conscience is put in Hitler's! In Germany I am a writer. I am hero of our great German Sigmund Freud...

[LOMAX laughs]

Braun: You laugh? Sigmund Freud has described the rest of time. Only a German could do this. *[To DANGERFIELD]* I was small boy when I discovered Freud and my mother's praises for reading this made me own him and love him.

Lomax: Isn't it a little unorthodox? Freud the Jew?...

Braun: So? I have heard the slanderers. They say that Herr Hitler may be part Jew. This is such disgrace. But how could we blame poor Adolf Hitler if he was, without knowing, scummed with bad blood? The Jews would thrive if, because of such conspiracy against our leader we sent him to Treblinka! You know, the Jews have this joke: I tell you...Kohn is walking down the street. He meets Goldstein who looks worried and preoccupied. To distract Goldstein, Kohn tells him that their mutual friend Davidsohn has died. Goldstein, through his stark eyes, looks at Kohn and says: "Well, if he got a chance to better himself..." You see? They will stop at nothing. Now I come back. *[To DANGERFIELD]* I tell you about my childhood lover, Freud. I tell you how the German is in the head of Hitler. It all comes from the unconscience... *[Struggling]*...the unconSCIOUSNESS...this is where it all comes from and this...being German comes from influences that make unconscience. That influence is Adolf Hitler and we all live in his unconscience and he guides us in our soil and responsibility.

[BRAUN seems on the point of collapse]

Lomax: *[Laughingly]* So that is what it is to be German!

Braun: Colonial, I speak to you but in the presence of this coward I don't like it. *[Indicates LOMAX]* I am surrounded with him and Italians. You know me Colonial it is the same, we have put our heads in. It doesn't matter which, the soil or Hitler's brain. It doesn't matter if we are Colonial Dangerfield or Lieutenant Braun....

[*CAPTAIN OPERARTI comes with shirt open*]

Operarti: [*Angrily*] Or Captain Vittorio Operarti, eh?

Braun: [*To DANGERFIELD*] We are nationals! [*About OPERARTI*] Look at him! He is not worked! He is not tired. He is not thirsted!...

Operarti: [*With accent*] I am a camel. This was told to me. I hear you Braun, I am listen. I stand over there. [*Points off*] Just by over there. You pretend I don't live? My mother say: this is these Nazis: they come to the Brenner Pass and don't believe we can hear them from the Alto Adige! They think if they cannot believe we can hear them that we are not there. In Alto Adige. But we are there, in Alto Adige and all over Italy. You know why?

[*Silence*]

Operarti: Because we are Italians!

Braun: [*To DANGERFIELD*] I suppose because his mother said so! We do not care!

Operarti: I know! That is why I want to talk to you Colonel as the boss. His Germans are taking our dirt!

Braun: Ah! The difference between the German and the Italian.

[*BRAUN goes off momentarily*]

[*He returns with a handful of dirt*]

Braun: [*Holding up hand*] Dirt. Whose is it?

[*Silence*]

Braun: [*Indicating DANGERFIELD*] It's his! Because we are [*Rubs his foot on ground*] on his soil. English dirt because English soil.

[*OPERARTI takes a small book out of his trousers. He flicks through it*]

Operarti: Aha! It might be English dirt because in England, but when Italian works it, it is Italian. [*Closes book*] Not for this case German!

Braun: [*Mockingly*] You see? He has book to tell him what to say! That is socialism! Duce Mussolini and Ciano are socialists!

Operarti: They are fascists! Wolves!

Braun: Lambs! They drink milk!

[*OPERARTI looks in book*]

Operarti: Hitler is a socialist!

[*Holds up book triumphantly*]

Braun: [*Enraged*] The Fuehrer is father of Nazism!

Operarti: [*Looks in book again*] National SOCIALISM!

[*Holds up book triumphantly*]

Braun: Nationalism!

Operarti: He is socialist lamb who looks like fascist wolf.

Braun: Nazism is the highest order of fascism.

[*OPERARTI looks in book*]

Operarti: Fascism is Italianism. There is no Nazi Italians.

[*Holds up book triumphantly*]

Braun: There are no Nazi Italians because if Italians could be Nazis there would be no Nazism!

Dangerfield: Gentlemen!

[*LOMAX is laughing loudly*]

Operarti: [*Outraged about LOMAX*] Look! He laughs.

Braun: About us!

Operarti: You know...I know... anyone will tell you in Italy, this Lomax here is coward.

[*BRAUN applauds*]

[*OPERARTI goes towards LOMAX*]

Operarti: In Italy, you know, he is a... you know - flower.

[*With his hand on hip, OPERARTI does effeminate walk*]

[*BRAUN advances on LOMAX quickly*]

Braun: [*Without pausing*] You can kick him!

[*BRAUN kicks Lomax who rolls over*]

[*OPERARTI spits*]

[*DANGERFIELD gets up with some difficulty. He takes his walking stick and waves it wildly*]

Dangerfield: Stop it!

[*BRAUN stops kicking*]

[*Silence*]

Dangerfield: Go back to your men.

[*BRAUN and OPERARTI begin to go off*]

[*BRAUN goes, OPERARTI pauses*]

Operarti: This is what the Duce told us: cowardice is on the same coin as cruelty. You notice, he did not cry out. D'Annunzio said, with a man like that that is sort of cruelty to himself. This my teacher told me D'Annunzio said. And he told us the man does not allow the passion to have expression. He is cold and ruthless. Then my teacher has said: our great genius of opera, Puccini, who you know before he died was fascist and writer of *La Tosca*, made in this great work, Scarpia, a traitor. He is dilettante about cruelty - cold even at the height of passion. He tortures the painter Mario before Tosca kills him. Lomax is a painter. He is Scarpia and Mario in one. It is possible. My teacher told me it is so. But if it is English, it is not Italian! Eia, eia, alala!

[*OPERARTI goes off*]

[*Silence*]

[*LOMAX calmly unrolls himself and dusts himself off*]

Dangerfield: [*Angrily*] Why didn't you fight back?

Lomax: That is the crux question.

Dangerfield: How far would you let him go?

[*Pause*]

Lomax: I'd let him pull my toenails off; tear off my genitals with his bare hands; pour hot wax in my ear...

Dangerfield: Quiet!

Lomax: [*Sitting on desk*] Do you think there is an English mind?

Dangerfield: [*Sitting at desk*] What ...do you mean...Yes!

Lomax: No! There OUGHT to be an English mind but there is not. If there was it might reason thus: Braun and Operarti are like children. They are the victims of a rabid mob parenthood. They have become mad too and play mad games - games that can kill. The English mind might reason that this madness must be resisted. It's infectious. We must be sure our children don't catch it. [*Pause. He gets up*] Do you think it's English to go from that position to reason that it's best to join them? [*He paces*] Just look over your shoulder Colonel! It's not important to the future of the world that we beat the Nazis. The world outside might look at us in Europe and find us indistinguishable one from the other. Chamberlain had a moustache; Hitler has one. For what it's worth, you may say this war is about the intolerance the one shows to the other's moustache!

[*LOMAX storms off*]

[*DANGERFIELD gets up with difficulty but decides not to go after him*]

Dangerfield: [*Shouting after LOMAX*] Lomax! [*Pause*] Lomax! You're right! This war is a continuation of the last one. And in the last one it was clear what to do with the people who wouldn't fight while those like me were out in the field losing our legs!

[*Silence*]

[*DANGERFIELD slumps into his chair*]

[*BRAUN comes on. He looks at DANGERFIELD and gestures at water*]

[*DANGERFIELD doesn't respond*]

[*BRAUN pours some water*]

[*He offers some to DANGERFIELD*]

[*DANGERFIELD declines*]

Braun: I admire you Colonial. [*He drinks*] I am sure your English leg is now flowering in the corner of some German field. That Lomax. [*He draws his hand across his throat*] He is just a waste of water.

[*Lights down*]

Scene Two

Scene: *Barn. Night.*

Hay or straw.

LOMAX is sleeping. There is a sketchpad etc near him.

KITTY comes on stealthily. She carries a travelling bag.

She sees LOMAX and pauses for a moment. She takes stock of where she is. She looks closely at LOMAX.

After a moment, she puts her bag down. She kneels and begins to pack straw into her clothing to simulate the appearance of pregnancy.

Completing this, she drapes herself across LOMAX's feet.

LOMAX stirs and pushes her off.

KITTY rolls off.

KITTY has an Irish accent.

Kitty: Christ! My belly!

[*LOMAX sits up startled*]

Lomax: What!....

Kitty: You surely killed my baby!

[*LOMAX is dazed*]

Lomax: What baby?

Kitty: The one in me belly! The one that belongs to Percy Smith!

[*LOMAX gets up. He paces*]

Lomax: Let me wake up.

[*KITTY lays down on her back motionless. She feel her belly*]

Kitty: No, the little one's still swimming in there, thank God.

[*LOMAX paces. He looks at her with disbelief. He pauses*]

Kitty: You'll know Percy Smith, then.

Lomax: [*Bemused*] What?

Kitty: You're a conscientious objector aren't you? The badge. Percy told me about it.

Lomax: I don't understand. What are you doing here?

Kitty: I'm looking for him. Percy Smith. You must know him.

Lomax: [*Still bewildered*] No.

[*Silence*]

[*LOMAX looks at KITTY with hostility*]

[*KITTY sits up. She takes a photo out. She shows photo to LOMAX*]

Kitty: Do you know him?

[*LOMAX takes photo a little reluctantly*]

Kitty: We shouldn't let the world estrange us.

Lomax: I don't know you. [*Gives photo back*] And I don't know him.

Kitty: Do you know the story of Ruth?

Lomax: I want to sleep. I sleep out here so I can be alone.

Kitty: Ruth married the son of a woman Naomi who'd come from a strange land and when he died and the poor Naomi was left grieving with no man, Ruth went back to her own country. To the land of Judah. And when Naomi's people saw how faithful Ruth had been to her, they accepted her as one of their own and even got married to the big fellow Boaz.

[*Silence*]

Kitty: They respected her even though she was a little strange woman in a foreign land.

Lomax: Is this a parable?

Kitty: I just think on some issues people can see eye to eye even if they've got different nationalities. Why are you here? Have you escaped?

[*LOMAX sits where he was sleeping*]

Lomax: No.

Kitty: But you're outside the camp.

Lomax: No, I'm not. The camp is open. There's no outside. And if there was you'd be safer inside.

Kitty: So...so I'm on the camp. I should be able to see Percy!

Lomax: No.

[*Silence*]

Kitty: He stopped writing. [*Suddenly angry*] Why would he do that? Why would he treat me like that? Because I'm Irish and he's English? I told him. I said: when I was a baby and we had the troubles and we were fighting the British, a conscientious objector would have seen as a supporter of the British occupation!

[*Silence*]

Lomax: [*Calmly but angrily*] The English require that it's a CONSCIENTIOUS objection.

Kitty: What?

Lomax: Because they want you to object to all war in order to object to one. Because otherwise you might be objecting to the stupidity of leaders. If your objection is a conscientious one it makes it look as if God has influenced you and that lets the English off the hook. They don't have to be responsible for your rebellion. It becomes God's. What they really want to do is find a way...[*Dismissively*] Christ!

Kitty: You remind me of someone.

[*LOMAX turns over*]

Kitty: What I don't get is: if this is not outside then where's everybody else? I mean, you may be inside the camp but you're outside in a way that all the inside are not.

Lomax: It's not outside. I told you. It may look outside because there's no identifiable inside. There's no fence.

Kitty: It's a metaphor! For British colonialism. For British treaties!

Lomax: I want to go to sleep. If you're staying here I want YOU to go to sleep!

[*Silence*]

[*KITTY gets her travelling bag. She picks up a dirty shawl. It's covered with paint. She holds it up. She takes shawl and bag together*]

Kitty: Do you think it would be possible for me to walk on in?

Wouldn't they have some compassion for a woman carrying an internee's baby?

Lomax: [*Sadly*] I don't know.

[*Silence*]

Kitty: Can you help me?

Lomax: No!

[*Silence*]

[*KITTY takes her blanket*]

Kitty: Would you like to share my blanket? It can still get cold.

[*Silence*]

Kitty: Do you mind if I share your hay?

[*LOMAX sighs*]

[*KITTY gets down with her back to him. She stuffs more hay into her 'belly'. She stops. She sits up and puts on shawl*]

Kitty: I couldn't help noticing there how you had a sketch pad and all the paraphernalia of the artist.

[*LOMAX rolls onto his back*]

Lomax: [*Points to shawl*] I use that to wipe my brushes.

Kitty: You see, it occured to me...if they let you outside in the night while all the others are inside, it might be because you're a painter. Would that be true? Perhaps, you see, if they can make these kind of allowances to let you out they may make the same kind of one to ...er...let you take me in.

Lomax: Sleep!

[*Silence*]

Kitty: I know who you remind me of.

[*LOMAX rolls back onto his side*]

Kitty: You remind me of Michael Collins. The Big Fellow they called him. A man who came and went as he pleased. I never knew him myself, of course, I was barely more than a baby when they shot him in the lonely land. He was coming down to Cork. Beal na mBlath. That was the name of the valley where they shot him. Just as night was falling. It means Mouth of The Flowers. You know, in all the years of the troubles when he was running the war against the British they could never catch him let alone shoot him. He used to come and go as he pleased. Sometimes coming through the dusk on a bicycle with the wings of his coat flying or just openly walking past Dublin Castle with the army out looking for him. But when it came to his own kind getting him... The Irish shot Michael. [*With disgust, a little aside*]. Christ, I know one thing. Percy's no Michael Collins!

[*Silence*]

Kitty: I remember my mother telling me: one day they heard that Collins was coming to town. When she looked at the crowd to see if she could pick him out, she saw this one handsome man and heard the accent and the chuckle and saw the twinkle in his eye and she knew that this was Collins.

[*Silence*]

[*KITTY sits up suddenly*]

Kitty: Do you need a model?

[*LOMAX is snoring*]

[*Lights down*]

Scene Three

Scene: *Same as Scene Two. Dawn.*

LOMAX and KITTY are sleeping.

BRAUN and OPERARTI can be heard talking off.

Braun: [*Without accent*] Operarti! Help me with this.

[*Silence*]

Braun: Operarti!

Operarti: [*With accent*] Why should I to speak your German. Why not Ribbentrop come to Rome? We speak German and the German cheats.

Braun: Cheats!

Operarti: Our sweet Ciano cheated by Ribbentrop.

Braun: Ribbentrop, Operarti, does not have to cheat the Ciano. After picking the white feather from his pouch, he could have pickled and dried his balls for parade ground whistles without a thought!

Operarti: Yes! Because he has no brain! Ow!

[*LOMAX and KITTY wake up*]

[*KITTY looks surprised and afraid*]

Operarti: White feathers! You speak like that vile violence because you know you have no alternative!

Braun: [*Angrily*] Just pick it up!

[*Silence*]

[*LOMAX and KITTY look up*]

[*LOMAX looks a little annoyed*]

[*BRAUN and OPERARTI come on with a coffin. BRAUN leads. As they come on they speak*]

[*LOMAX lays back down. KITTY the same. They pretend to sleep*]

Operarti: Will you tell me why we must bring this here?

Braun: Because we don't want it left outside where people may see it and think it's being used.

[*OPERARTI stops*]

[*The coffin drops from BRAUN's hands. They don't see LOMAX and KITTY*]

Operarti: That make no sense!

Braun: Why did you stop!

[*BRAUN bends down to pick up his end of the coffin. He puts his hands under coffin*]

[*As he does, OPERARTI drops his end and stands on it triumphantly*]

Operarti: [*As he gets on coffin*] Because it make no sense!

[*BRAUN lets out a cry of pain*]

[*OPERARTI gets off coffin*]

[*BRAUN jumps up and down shaking his hand*]

Braun: Christ! It's not supposed to make sense! It's supposed to be done!

Operarti: A coffin must be used. People know this. It doesn't matter if they see it and think it's being used. What you should worry is if they see it used and then see it again! Because a coffin used should be buried. And this one, it is used and not buried!

Braun: Very well, we're pretending it's a wheelbarrow. [*Mimicks using wheelbarrow*]. You see? We don't leave wheelbarrows out at night.

Operarti: This is because it might rain.

Braun: Pick it up!

[BRAUN stands with his back to the front of the coffin. He squats to pick to pick it up]

[As he does, OPERARTI quickly and angrily lifts his end]

[BRAUN is hit in the back and overbalances]

Operarti: [*Without accent*] I refuse to speak another word that is not in my own Italian!

[BRAUN falls back]

[OPERARTI drops his end]

[BRAUN fall on his back and hurts it. He lets out a cry]

Braun: [*Without accent*] My back! [*With accent*] We have had to drag you into this age of steel, this age of men like Stalin. No more! This is where we draw the line! YOU will get at the front!

[They change places]

[BRAUN picks his end up very quickly]

Braun: Hup!

[OPERARTI sits on his end]

[The coffin falls on BRAUN's foot. BRAUN cries out]

Operarti: [*Without accent*] I've just seen something I wouldn't have thought possible.

[BRAUN goes to OPERARTI threateningly]

Operarti: [*Without accent*] Look, Lomax in the hay with a girl.

[BRAUN stops. He looks at LOMAX and KITTY with surprise. His surprise turns to anger]

[BRAUN goes close to LOMAX and KITTY]

[BRAUN goes to OPERARTI and puts an arm around him]

Braun: [*Without accent*] Operarti, you know what I believe.

Operarti: [*With accent*] No.

Braun: What? Why not? I've told you enough!

Operarti: To know what you believe I would have to know why you believe it. But I do not even know why I believe what I believe!

Braun: What!

Operarti: I believe in d'Annunzio but I have never read him. I love d'Annunzio.

Braun: [*Whispering, without accent*] Listen! Nothing, as far as I'm concerned, in this world - and perhaps what you've just said is proof of it - is rational. Rationalism is an illusion. A dangerous one. That's how I can understand THAT. [*Points to LOMAX and KITTY*] A night in the hay - that's a saying - but who's ever done it? LOMAX! Only Lomax isn't supposed to do it! [*Angrily*] Not only is he not supposed to do it because nobody actually does it, he's not supposed to do it because he's not supposed to do it! Understand? So what do we do? Do we let him go on doing what he's not supposed to do, or do we act?

Operarti: What do you mean?

Braun: Finish him off! Here and now. And [*Pause. He looks at KITTY*] We could fuck the girl.

[*Silence*]

Braun: [*Angrily*] What's the matter? You don't object do you? YOU'RE not an objector. That is well known about Operarti. he did not object to coming to war even though he knew deep down his own Duce didn't want the war. But because the Duce - under the influence of Adolf Hitler - reasoned it was unavoidable, then Operarti does not object. Nor does he object to being a prisoner of war...

Operarti: I don't object but I won't do it. That is not objecting – that is being intelligent.

Braun: How!

Operarti: [*Still with accent*] Dangerfield loves him.

Braun: What! What do you mean 'loves'?

Operarti: I don't know. For Dangerfield, Lomax is absolute English.

Braun: But he is a conscientious objector!

Operarti: You cannot prove that. There is more evidence that he is English than that he is conscientious objector. Dangerfield believes so. That is why he allows him...his night in hay. We cannot kill him! If we kill him Dangerfield will kill us. He would do it. The English are barbarians.

[*Silence*]

[*BRAUN paces*]

Braun: [*Still without accent*] What shall we do?

Operarti: We can only object.

Braun: [*Horrified*] Object!

Operarti: We must tell Dangerfield that we cannot accept this kind of behaviour any longer. Come.

[*OPERARTI begins to go*]

Braun: Do you have any idea of the kind of opportunity you're letting slip here?

[*Pause*]

Operarti: I was baby when Mussolini came to power. I don't know what ideas are. I never had any. [*Short pause*] Except once I have the idea that my sister's boyfriend was flower and another time I had idea about how to cheat the lottery. But neither one came to anything.

[*They go off*]

[*LOMAX sits up*]

[*KITTY sits up*]

Kitty: I was so frightened. What's the coffin for?

Lomax: Nothing.

Kitty: Did you understand what they were saying?

Lomax: Yes.

Kitty: What were they saying?

Lomax: Nothing.

[*He gets up*]

Lomax: I think you should know that those men will report your presence here.

Kitty: Will I be arrested?

[*LOMAX begins putting his things together*]

Lomax: I'm going to leave you.

Kitty: If I'm arrested, that would be a way to see Percy.

[*Silence*]

Lomax: If you're arrested, they'll rape you. They'll cut out your baby or some such devilish thing.

Kitty: I was forgetting where I was. This IS England. The English would do that. [*She pulls at LOMAX*] You see, you must help me!

Lomax: I am English.

Kitty: No, but you're fighting the English. I know you. You're not someone struggling with his conscience - you're fighting. You may be the only man in England who's really fighting the fascists.

Lomax: I'm not fighting anything. I'm an English painter.

[*KITTY gets up. She holds her 'belly' up*]

Kitty: This baby, when it grows, will have to struggle. It'll have to struggle against it's own fascists - the one's that'll be strutting about its little brain. Just as the Free State had to struggle against Eoin O'Duffy and his blueshirts who came from the ranks of the Free State itself. It'll have to struggle against the hatred it has for its own kind. That's what you're doing. You're fighting against the Nazism in the English. I can see it because I'm Irish. We've been through it all. We all should have this struggle in ourselves. I'm fighting it by the minute. In meself.

Lomax: [*About to go*] Have you come to kill your husband?

Kitty: Jesus, he's not me husband! [*Pause. Angrily*] How could you say a thing like that?

[*She sits down defiantly*]

Kitty: I'm staying put! I'm not going to be pushed around anymore by anyone who thinks I'm just a stupid Irish whore.

[*LOMAX goes off*]

Kitty: [*Shouting after him*] If I had a gun I'd shoot the lot of yous!

[*Lights down*]

Scene Four

Scene: *DANGERFIELD is marching in a circle.*

His false leg insists on presenting itself as in a German goosestep.

Braun: [*Off. With accent*] Colonial!

[*DANGERFIELD suddenly stops. He seems annoyed, embarrassed*]

[*BRAUN comes on*]

Braun: You are practising eh? Rehearsing?

Dangerfield: Practising? Rehearsing? What are you talking about?

Braun: [*Marching*] You were...I saw you...this marching.

Dangerfield: [*Angrily*] I was not! I was exercising my leg!

Braun: [*Still marching*] Your leg? But I thought this leg was wooden.

Dangerfield: Not the wooden one. The other one! You see?

[*Begins walking/marching again*]

[*OPERARTI marches on*]

Operarti: I have always like to drill. It is beautiful. The women like it.

[*DANGERFIELD suddenly stops*]

Dangerfield: This is absurd! Stop it!

[*The others stop*]

Dangerfield: Why aren't you in the field?

[*Short silence*]

Braun: There is a woman in the barn with Lomax.

Dangerfield: What?

Operarti: [*With accent as before*] We didn't want to object but we
have to say something about it.

Dangerfield: Why?

Braun: What?

Dangerfield: If you didn't want to object, why do you have to say
something about it?

Braun: No, well...this is not exactly correct. Operarti has it wrong
again. You see, I was coming close to violence and we thought:
better than violence we should tell you.

Dangerfield: You mean: make an objection rather than use violence.

Operarti: Well...objection is...you know...a bit strong the word.

[*DANGERFIELD paces*]

Dangerfield: [*Holding back anger*] I see...so you were going to use
violence against Lomax because he's stuffing some bird in the
barn. Is that it?

Braun: Yes.

Operarti: No.

[*They look at each other*]

Dangerfield: You mean 'yes and no' to the stuffing?

Both: Yes.

Dangerfield: Aha! I see. Braun wants to believe Lomax is stuffing the
girl because he himself wants to...perhaps rape the girl and
Lomax, having already done the act, mitigates Braun's horrific
intentions, while Operarti...Operarti doesn't want to believe Lomax
is doing it because his boiling Virgilian blood couldn't bare the
shame of his envy. So: Is Lomax shagging the girl or not?

Operarti: I tell you: no.

Dangerfield: [*Stopping at OPERARTI*] Why so sure?

Operarti: Because the girl is pregnant.

[*Silence*]

Braun: How do you know!

Operarti: I could see!

[*Pause*]

Braun: Well...he could do it from the back.

Operarti: [*Shocked*] Do the English do this?

Dangerfield: O, yes. O, yes, the English can do this!

Braun: [*Happily*] So!

Dangerfield: If there was a way to the centre of the world the English would find it. If there was a way to inhabit that centre, the English would do it. When there was free world in the west the English found it and claimed it. Through the front door. When tyrants barred front doors in the east, the English found back doors. They do what they do from back or front. But in this case...in this case we would be men of straw to speculate and, who knows, the woman may be a straw cat!

Braun: I understand this!

Operarti: But is it right, even if Lomax not shags or even if he shags and she is the wife, for her to be here? For him to shag?

Dangerfield: I would be a fool to condemn Lomax where condemnation in this case should be absence of what we are condemning.

[*Silence*]

[*BRAUN paces, thinking*]

Operarti: You mean you would condemn him for not married?

Dangerfield: From whatever his passion's position.

Braun: [*Stopping*] You mean whether he shagged but married or not shagged and not?

Dangerfield: [*Impatiently*] Not and not. Yes.

Operarti: [*Thinking*] Not and not?

Braun: It mean: you condemn the not shagging. But Operarti says he not shagged!

Dangerfield: Ah! But I speak as an English man-of-war. If Operarti is right then Lomax is even more English than I thought. He is more English than the English man-of-war and that is English beyond condemnation. Go back to your fields.

[*DANGERFIELD struts off*]

Braun: [*To OPERARTI, without accent*] You know, Goebbels is a master of propaganda. If your mother-in-law cheated you out of your home, he could talk her into giving it back. If a judge convicted an innocent man, Goebbels could convince him the man was guilty. A monk he could talk out of masturbating and he could make a virgin tear at her own cheating hymen. We're the same breed he and I. But here I have allowed you to talk me into restraint with the girl while the Englishman has defended the coward and prepared the way for his own night in the hay!.

Operarti: [*With accent*] No! I have watched the colonel. He is straight-laced. He is tied to being England. In England they shag only for to make the baby. The Colonel's life is like algebra. Today his x's are Lomax, only tomorrow, maybe next year, will his x's be sex.

Braun: [*With disgust*] Operarti! You do not belong to the age you live in. Your romanticism is already dead.

[*BRAUN goes off leaving OPERARTI looking glum and alone*]

[*Lights down*]

Scene Five

Scene: *The barn. Hay.*

KITTY is singing the song: "O, My Baby...".

She is sewing up a piece of material into a pouch. Into the pouch she is stuffing hay (straw)

BRAUN comes on a little and watches.

He is unseen by KITTY.

BRAUN sees KITTY take hay from her 'belly'.

When she finishes stitching the pouch, she stands up and holds it to her belly.

Braun: So!

[*KITTY jumps*]

[*BRAUN goes to her*]

Braun: [*With accent. About pouch*] What is this?

Kitty: It's a...it's a pillow.

Braun: A pillow! Ha! It is your baby!

[*Silence*]

Braun: You are not pregnant.

[*He snatches pillow from her*]

Braun: [*With accent still*] So, Lomax, he has done the shagged you!

Kitty: You're not taking it from me!

Braun: [*Without accent*] Lomax must have put her up to this pregnancy! He would do it knowing that it would incline us towards thinking that he hasn't touched her.

Kitty: You're just like the English aristocracy hiding behind your tongue!

Braun: [*With accent*] Lomax, he has put this up you!

Kitty: He has not!

[*The 'baby' breaks*]

Kitty: O, no!

[*She begins immediately to put it together again*]

Kitty: Now he'll know. [*Tearfully*] I was just getting him to trust me. To sympathise with me. I was just beginning to believe...to know what it could be like to have a man care for you because you've been impregnated with life.

[*Pause*]

Braun: [*Directly to audience. Without accent*] So Lomax couldn't have done it: He would know the baby is straw. [*Pause*]. But the haughty, proper English would have done it. They make babies and don't care whether they're made of flesh or straw. A matter of indifference: the first cause in the chain whose effect is a baby, is no more significant than a piss. Ironically, this cavalier carelessness is seen as ...an endearing quality of the nobility. In the world's eye, the proper English, having become noble, are then seen as carers after the interests of babies! Even though, to complete an idea, they would raze a Cologne or a Hamburg, mothers, babies: the lot! So if Lomax hasn't done it [*indicates KITTY*] which we know to be the case, then Lomax cannot be proper English. He must be improper English.

[*BRAUN seems suddenly struck by an idea*]

Braun: Whilst the proper English SEEM noble, it's the improper English who care for babies!

[*BRAUN helps KITTY re-stuff 'baby'*]

Braun: [*With accent*] If you want baby, I care.

[*KITTY looks at BRAUN sceptically*]

Kitty: You care? Supposing I don't? Supposing I just want the baby so I can stay?

Braun: [*With accent*] Maybe you do not want baby but only appearance of it. Maybe...

Kitty: Maybe as long as this is a secret you have a special power over me.

Braun: [*With a shrug*] Yes.

Kitty: But I'm the one who wants to keep the secret.

Braun: [*Without accent*] It is a fantastic paradox.

Kitty: Why'd you speak so that I can't understand you? If you're planning to rape me it's the same whatever the language.

Braun: [*With accent*] But what you say: you are responsible for whatever.

Kitty: [*Aggressively*] Yes! I could even be responsible for me own rape!

Braun: [*With accent*] But why do you speak of rape?

Kitty: Because there's no other way you're going to be doing it!

[*Silence*]

[*BRAUN gets up suddenly*]

Braun: [*Angrily*] I want your baby.

Kitty: So you finally came out with it. Mind you, I didn't expect you to call it anything other than a fuck...

Braun: [*With accent*] No! I do not want this! I could not now...I am confused...[*Without accent*] If Lomax DOES care about babies...I can't think!...There must be a way to use...

[*BRAUN goes back to stuffing 'baby'. He works quickly*]

Braun: [*With accent*] I will not rape to you to keep your baby. To keep your baby you must give it to me.

[*Pause*]

[*KITTY picks up 'baby' and thrusts it into his arms*]

Kitty: Have it! Now you tell me how I'm keeping it. [*Angrily*]. That's the language of brass-faced generals and chicken-legged politicians!

[*BRAUN thrusts it back into her arms with greater force*]

Braun: [*With accent*] I will tell you...at some time, I will tell you when I want it...Quiet!

[*They listen*]

Braun: The step: do you hear it?

Kitty No.

Braun: Hurry! Come on!

[*They fill 'baby'*]

Braun: Lay down.

Kitty: What?

[*Braun pushes her down. He lifts her skirt and puts "baby" up astride her*]

Braun: [*Without accent*] I'm giving her a baby! Christ! If Goebbels could see me now!

Kitty: Why do you blather on like that?

[*BRAUN pulls skirt down*]

Braun: [*With accent*] Done.

[*BRAUN rushes off*]

[*KITTY sits up*]

[*After a brief moment DANGERFIELD comes on. He carries water in a receptacle*]

Dangerfield: You must be thirsty.

[*KITTY looks at him with surprise*]

Dangerfield: We're desperate for rain. The English have become desperados! [*He gives a forced laugh*]

[*He gives her a drink*]

Kitty: You always were.

[*DANGERFIELD looks thunderstruck*]

Dangerfield: Pardon?

Kitty: I said the English always were desperados.

[*She drinks greedily*]

Dangerfield: [*Horror struck*] You're Irish?

Kitty: I am. Sure.

[*Short silence*]

Dangerfield: [*Turning away*] The Irish used to be British.

[*KITTY stands up angrily*]

Kitty: The Irish were never British!

Dangerfield: [*Also angrily, going away from her*] Why didn't the Irish want to be British? Why didn't they want to be English! Why do people NOT WANT TO BE ENGLISH!

Kitty: Would the English want to be Irish?

[*Silence*]

[*KITTY puts her blanket over the coffin and sits on it. She speaks as she does this*]

Kitty: I'll tell you why the Irish, or anyone else for that matter, who's not English doesn't want to BE English. You've got no sense of hospitality! I'll tell you about it: when I first set foot in Britain, at Liverpool, I was overcome by six English soldiers. It was a night crossing and my nerves were high. As we spotted the harbour, the sun began to rise. I got off with my sack of clothes and scarf upon my head and I was hardly through customs when they got me there in the early morning. Can you imagine that? I come from the land of Moab where civilization is like the rocks in the sand around Jabesh Gilead, across the waters to the land of high hopes and promise, milk and honey, and there in the early morning, this frail girl gets raped by six brute soldiers. They're even worse when they set foot in YOUR country. Then, they take away YOUR right to be hospitable. Don't talk to me about the English - I've had breakfast with them!

[*DANGERFIELD turns to her*]

Dangerfield: You're pregnant.

Kitty: What of it?

Dangerfield: Do you know who I am?

Kitty: You look like a bookmaker.

Dangerfield: I'm the officer in charge of the camp. Dangerfield.

[*Silence*]

Dangerfield: You know Lomax?

Kitty: I met him.

[*DANGERFIELD goes towards her.*]

Dangerfield: He didn't....did he?

Kitty: Didn't what? Didn't do what those soldiers did? No.

[*DANGERFIELD offers her a drink.*]

[*She drinks.*]

Dangerfield: He wouldn't. He's too English.

Kitty: Too English? Jesus, I wouldn't say that. That's your soldiers! I'd say it was because he's a conscientious objector. They have a general slant of mind towards doing things that don't upset people.

Dangerfield: No!

Kitty: What?

Dangerfield: Why are you here?

Kitty: There's a man - Percy Smith.

Dangerfield: A conscientious objector?

Kitty: Yes.

Dangerfield: He's been here since the beginning of the war?

Kitty: Yes.

Dangerfield: Previously, you were content to wait at home, until the war finished, for this man to return.

Kitty: Yes.

Dangerfield: But isn't it true that he's stopped writing to you? That that has made you upset and caused you to come here to look for him?

Kitty: If your husband's a fisherman and he's gone out to get food for the family and boat capsizes, you don't refuse to go and look for him just because you've missed your tea!

[*Silence*]

Dangerfield: That's his baby?

Kitty: It is.

Dangerfield: I can help you see him.

Kitty: "Help" me! You could order it! You could just say: Smith, there's a lady here come to see you. WITH YOUR BABY. It's compassionate consideration. You could call it conscientious subjection!

Dangerfield: You want to see Smith and I want to see Lomax.

Kitty: Surely you can see him whenever you want to.

Dangerfield: I want to see the real Lomax. I want to find out whether or not he IS a conscientious objector. If you can show me, for example, that Lomax is NOT a conscientious objector then I will let you see Smith.

Kitty: And if I show that, you'll have him shipped off to the front line and I'd have his death on me conscience.

Dangerfield: Not at all. If you can show me this, it'll prove to me that he is as English as he seems!

Kitty: But he IS as English as he seems!

Dangerfield: I mean he seems too English to be a conscientious objector. He doesn't mix with the others. [*He paces with walking stick*] There are many born in England in whom conscientious objection is merely a lapse of Englishness. These can be brought back to the mother culture. Lomax is not one of these. In Lomax Englishness hasn't lapsed. I need to have confirmed what I believe to be true: that it is not possible to be English AND a conscientious objector.

Kitty: [*Scoffingly*] You can't be English and a conscientious objector? [*Pause. Angrily*] If you ask me, it may be the only thing you English have got left to save you from a bloody good stoning. You Vikings have battered down one too many door of the temple. Maybe it's the objectors who are the real English.

Dangerfield: [*Very angry*] No! I'll tell you what they are.

[*DANGERFIELD goes close to KITTY*]

Dangerfield: [*About his false leg*] Feel that!

[*KITTY feels it*]

Kitty: It's wood.

Dangerfield: Yes! That's the conscientious objector: the wooden leg of the body politic; of the state bellicose. The conscientious objector is death within the system; the splinter in the visionary eye of the warrior. Life is a dance with death. The conscientious objector is the wooden leg which causes you to stumble. Worse than that: the conscientious objector is the black leg in the struggle when we need unity to meet the enemy. We don't want to humble our people; we are not looking for their defeat; we don't aim to de-Christianise them; to make them murderers; to send them out to the five continents of the world with daggers; to disperse like smoke their power or burst the balloon of their glory. We love our people; we are proud of our people; we want our people to go into the world and be loved; for our people to be victorious so that the world becomes like us: noble and gracious; happy and glorious, to reign over the world with peace and with Englishness!

[*He falls silent suddenly*]

Kitty: What if Lomax is not English?

[*Silence*]

Kitty: What if Lomax is a conscientious objector?

Dangerfield: Then I want you to show me THAT.

Kitty: And then I will see Percy?

Dangerfield: You will.

[*He marches off*]

[*KITTY stands up and lifts her "baby"*]

Kitty: Well, at least I'm on the camp, Percy. Even if I don't discover the real Lomax - who I couldn't care less about - I may, in some dark, in some accident, come face to face with you.

[*Lights down*]

[*END OF PART ONE*]

Part Two

Scene Six

Scene: *Some time later.*

There is an easel with a canvas on it.

This is covered with a cloth.

BRAUN and OPERARTI come on stealthily.

Braun: [*Without accent*] Vittorio. This will hurt I know, but I must show you. He is painting a painting of Mussolini called Death of Titan.

Operarti [*With accent*] Death?

Braun: Sssshhhh.

Operarti: Of Titan. [*Pause*] Does this 'Titan' honour the Duce?

Braun: Well, you'd think so. Lomax believes it honours himself. You know with his neo-classical style. That is what his Englishness is, you see. But what is neo-classical about this!

[*BRAUN takes cover from painting*]

[*OPERARTI jumps back with a gasp, crossing himself*]

Braun: Upside down with his body falling into his hat!

[*Silence*]

[*OPERARTI paces*]

Operarti: I believe in the Duce; that God made him.

Braun: God had no choice.

Operarti: I believe in all things Italian; that God made us .

Braun: Spoken boldly! - In German.

Operarti: I believe in the Fascio di Combattimento.

Braun: Heil!

Operarti: I believe that the Duce is virile: that all Italians are virile and that is what Duce and God want.

Braun: Making babies is the great Italian art in the Fascist era.

Operarti: I believe it!

[*OPERARTI indicates painting*]

Operarti: Do you believe this is political?

[*BRAUN nods affirmatively*]

Operarti: I don't know what politics are! We never had any!

Braun: With the Duce you never needed any.

Operarti: I don't know what ideas are - I've never had any - except once I had the idea that my sister's boy friend was a flower and another I had an idea about how to cheat the lottery but not one came to anything. [*Passionately*] I love d'Annunzio even though I have never never read him!

Braun: As I will be loved!

Operarti: I am not sure about the war. I know the Duce did not want it...

Braun: But he's asked you to fight it.

Operarti: And so I do not object.

Braun: Do you know why! Because in Italy you are all a bit of Mussolini!

Operarti Yes! I believe it! If Mussolini died, a bit of me would die!

Braun: [*Indicating painting*] So you object to this!

Operarti: I believe it!

[*OPERARTI takes out a sharp object like a knife.*]

Operarti: This is asking me to die!

[*OPERARTI strikes painting and damages it*]

Braun: Bravo, Operarti!

[*Silence*]

Braun: How do you feel?

Operarti: Alive!

Braun: You'd like to do it again wouldn't you?

[*OPERARTI is tense*]

Braun: It was all your frustration flooding out.

[*Pause*]

Braun: You are frustrated...sexually.

[*OPERARTI looks at BRAUN sceptically*]

Braun: It's true, I know, I've studied it. Let me explain: Mussolini is upside down which makes him, symbolically, a woman. You have taken your knife, which is a symbol for your penis, and stabbed him in the belly. Does it make sense? Think about it. If Mussolini represents the woman, then he/she is unyielding both in the sense that he is only a figure in paint, but also in the sense that like all women at this time for you, for me, for everyone on the camp, he is unavailable. And, of course, he is a man. And perhaps...perhaps there is even a sense in which you are blaming Mussolini for putting you in this situation. But that, of course, is bye the bye. The main point is that Mussolini is the woman you cannot have. So! You need a woman. If you don't have a woman soon ...who knows...it could develop into a fetish for stabbing effigies of the Duce! The mind under stress...Ach! Ask yourself: is there a woman you could have?

[*OPERARTI looks worried and preoccupied*]

Operarti: I don't... know...

Braun: The Irish girl. Kitty!

Operarti: What?

Braun: Cover up the Duce and I'll explain.

[*OPERARTI covers painting*]

Braun: You know in 1919 when the fascists got only 4,000 votes, the newspaper 'Avanti' said that Mussolini was a political corpse. His coffin was paraded up and down the streets of Milan. But he was a fascist. What is a fascist?

[*OPERARTI looks bewildered*]

Braun: He is a fighting machine! So they fought. They beat up the opposition in the streets, in their homes, in the cafes, in the schools, in the factories; they murdered Matteotti...anything, anything was done to win. Under threat the fascist fights until he is victorious. Using any tactic. Now then, the Italian, after he is a fascist, he is what?

[*OPERARTI looks bemused*]

[*BRAUN does a pumping gesture with his arm*]

Braun: He is a loving, shagging machine. [*Pause*] The Italian is the fascist lover. In other words, if they are saying that you're a sexual corpse, and if the way you live; your own actions; your frustrations suggest this is true, then you must fight back and use every tactic. You must have Kitty.

Operarti: How?

[*BRAUN looks off*]

Braun: She's coming!

Operarti: [*Panicking*] So soon! What I shall do? What I should to say?

Braun: Get her on your side. Get her away from Lomax - to sympathise with you. Tell her... I don't know...tell her that Lomax has been going round the camp telling everyone he's shagging her! I'll hide!

Operarti: It is true he says this?

Braun: [*Going off to hide*] Yes!

[*OPERARTI peeps beneath cloth at painting*]

[*KITTY comes on*]

[*OPERARTI jumps back operatically*]

Operarti: [*With accent. With a gasp*] Miss Kitty! You have caught me!

Kitty: Caught you?

Operarti: It is my Italian fascist blood. I mean lover blood...it boils.

Kitty: I don't know what you're talking about. Have you seen Mr Lomax? He's supposed to be painting me.

Operarti: [*Surprised*] Painting you? But is this allowed? You know, if the camp commander...

Kitty: No, it's alright. He's given a dispensation. I think he's got a soft spot for the big fella.

Operarti: [*With increased interest*] Who is this "big fellow"?

Kitty: Lomax.

Operarti: You know...Please sit. You have the baby; you must be careful. [*Angrily*] This Lomax, if in Italy would be shot. He lies!

[*KITTY sits*]

Kitty: Lies? About what?

Operarti: Lying is the worst thing. Shall I get you some water? It is even hot for me.

[*He looks around*]

Operarti: Lomax must have water if he is painter. [*Searching*] You know, I was in school, only a small child when Il Duce became our leader. Once, he comes to our small school in Genoa. You know Genoa? It is beautiful. It is like port at the gates of history. He told us this story.

[*He finds a large container of water*]

Operarti: Here is water. Mama mia! How can this be? Look how much is here? So many people have no water and Lomax has so much!

Kitty: Mr Lomax must have royalty in his family!

[*OPERARTI sighs*]

Operarti: Anyway...

[*OPERARTI looks for something to use as a cup*]

Operarti: Mussolini came to this school to tell us how important not to lie. He said that when he was young boy, he cut down cherry tree...

[*KITTY looks at OPERARTI incredulously*]

[*OPERARTI finds a container to use as a cup*]

[*He pours KITTY out a drink*]

[*He kneels on one leg before her offering her the drink*]

Operarti: When his father asked if he cut down tree, he told the truth. He had to he said no matter what it would cost him.

[*KITTY drinks*]

Kitty: It's a lie.

Operarti: [*Shocked*] What!

Kitty: It was George Washington.

Operarti: George Wash..ton. Who is this?

Kitty: George Washington. The first president of the United States of America. He was the one with the tree.

Operarti: [*Jumping up offended*] But that is lie!

Kitty: You mean I'm lying?

Operarti: No, no not you. If you have been taught lie to be truth then how can you know it is lie?

[*Silence*]

Operarti: [*Sadly*] You believe me I don't lie?

Kitty: I don't believe you'd be lying and knowing you were.

[*OPERARTI paces agitatedly*]

Operarti: Well I believe...Lomax, he lies. About you.

Kitty: [*Raised eyebrows*] About me? I'm surprised he even thinks about me.

[*OPERARTI holds her by the arms*]

Operarti: You must not say this like this! It is important that this is true!

[*KITTY doesn't resist OPERARTI*]

[*She gets up but ensures that he keeps his distance*]

Kitty: You mean important that we THINK it's true. Even if it's not?

Operarti: [*Confused*] No, why? It IS true.

Kitty: What is?

[*Silence*]

[*OPERARTI is reluctant to tell her*]

Operarti: You see...I don't believe that he...You are preg...the baby, you know...he said...he said that he will...has been making...you know...

[*KITTY moves towards OPERARTI a little playfully*]

Kitty: You mean having sexual intercourse with me?

[*OPERARTI gasps*]

[*He takes his arms from her*]

[*He crosses himself*]

Operarti: This is what he says.

[*He takes hold of KITTY again and kisses her*]

[*He finishes kissing her*]

Kitty: It's a lie.

[*She keeps OPERARTI at arms length*]

Operarti: [*Softly*] I have never felt a baby in a belly before. It is very soft.

[*KITTY turns away from OPERARTI*]

Kitty: You're like a child. Lomax is a hundred years old. He wouldn't say it.

Operarti: It is what I said. But he has been telling the whole camp.

[*KITTY sits still turned away from OPERARTI*]

Kitty: Did he tell you himself?

[*OPERARTI speaks as if pleading*]

Operarti: No...not himself to my face...

Kitty: [*Turning to him with mock anger*] What then! His to someone else's face or someone else to yours?

Operarti: [*Helplessly. Confused*] Someone else has told me and I believed him.

[*Pause*]

Kitty: Why should you believe him?

Operarti: [*Baffled*] But why not ? Why should he lie to me? I would not hurt him that he told me truth.

Kitty: [*Sympathetically*] You wouldn't even hurt him if he told you a lie.

Operarti: This may be true. I don't know. In Italy there is no lies. Only truth.

Kitty: [*Genuine anger*] That's propaganda!

Operarti: [*A little confused*] Propaganda? Propaganda, it is English lie.

Kitty: Ah!

[*KITTY gets up. She paces going away from OPERARTI*]

Kitty: Lomax is English. You say he's telling lies. So what he's supposed to be saying is propaganda!

Operarti: [*Confused*] Yes?

Kitty: But we all know that propaganda's not the truth and because we all know that it can't be a lie. The intention of a lie is to deceive you. Propaganda is just another weapon in war - it's to win the fight.

[*OPERARTI looks lost*]

[*KITTY walks towards OPERARTI*]

Kitty: So Lomax's claims would not have the intention of deceiving you like a lie but would have some other purpose.

[*KITTY stands face to face with OPERARTI*]

Kitty: So you may be lying to me by deceiving yourself without knowing it.

[*OPERARTI falls to his knees before her*]

Operarti: Miss Kitty...it is terrible things to say...it is terrible things to tell you and you have this baby...it is all terrible...

Kitty: It's not nice for sure.

Operarti: But I can't help!... You know, I never had wife. [*Pause*] The great Italian art is for making babies and I never had wife!

[*KITTY laughs*]

Kitty: Who told you that?

[*She pats and strokes OPERARTI's head*]

Operarti: What?

Kitty: The great Italian art!

[*OPERARTI looks bemused*]

[*LOMAX comes on*]

Lomax: What's this great Italian art, Operarti?

[*OPERARTI stands and faces LOMAX defiantly*]

Operarti: I have one question for you. What is more important: a man's thirst or a man's painting?

[*LOMAX picks up water. He drinks*]

Lomax: A man's paintings.

[*OPERARTI is enraged*]

Operarti: That is a lie! You know it! [*To KITTY*] You see! He will lie just to mock me and others who are thirsty. A man has no paintings without water but worst: he has no life. [*To KITTY*]. Now you see how he can lie and for only cheap reason. What if the reason was to gain much more? You will have it coming, Lomax. And when you get it you will see.

[*OPERARTI storms off*]

[*LOMAX takes cover from painting. He sees it's damaged but doesn't react*]

[*KITTY jumps up when she sees damage*]

Kitty: [*Going to painting*] Your painting! He must have done it!

[*LOMAX takes down painting in silence*]

Kitty: Aren't you annoyed? Jesus!

Lomax: What should I do? Declare war on the Italians?

Kitty: You're not real are you? Nothing effects you. Nothing makes a difference. It makes no difference that I'm here.

[*Silence*]

Kitty: You're like the painting. It's not real is it? It's not true?

[*LOMAX puts another canvas on easel*]

Lomax: You mean because it's upside down? I agree. I don't like it.

[*LOMAX takes chair and places it where he wants KITTY to sit*]

Lomax: An advantage of all this sun is that you can calculate your light requirements quite accurately.

[*LOMAX indicates that she should sit in chair*]

Kitty: [*Testily*] And another thing is that it might distract the onlooker when she wonders about how cool you are with your damaged art. She might think it's because you've got more water than anyone else! I don't know why I'm doing this!

Lomax: Stick your belly out. I want the full effect of its pathos. New life in the midst of death.

Kitty: What death?

Lomax: Well, strictly speaking, what new life? It's unborn.

[*LOMAX takes up charcoal stick*]

Kitty: While we're on the subject of strictly speaking, do you ever do it? I mean in the sense of strictly speaking the truth?

[*LOMAX begins sketching*]

Lomax: "The truth" isn't the best way to describe it. Representation is better.

Kitty: Are we talking about the same thing or is this some private theory of yours?

Lomax: Maybe. It's the painter in me! Attempts to discover the reality in the components of painting - what makes it up: colour, line, shape - are, perhaps, necessarily abstract. These abstractions are considered to reveal the truth while more representational painting is dismissed as thoughtless. Merely reflecting, in a banal way, the world we live in. I disagree. I believe if you have something to say about the world we live in, you say it as directly as possible in a way that people can understand. Abstraction obscures. For me the decisive moment came in 1934 when Gottfried Benn in Germany wrote that he wanted to fuse Expressionism with Nazism in the way that Marinetti's Futurism was a part of Italian Fascism. Then I knew that expressions of truth come from the truth itself not from the expression. For me the truth in art is representation.

[*KITTY looks bewildered*]

Kitty: Jesus! If that's all you can remember from the last 10 years...! I think you might be hiding behind all those 'isms'. I wouldn't have thought HOW you say something is so important but why you want to say it. Is there any way that you consider that the representation might be more true than the truth? I mean, do you think, for example, supposing a woman looked pregnant but wasn't pregnant but she looked pregnant in whatever way it could be contrived because that reflected her true feelings about herself: would it be truer to say that she was pregnant or that she wasn't?

Lomax: [*Still sketching*] If a painting was of a mother and child, its truth would lie in what it represents of the universe it inhabits. Anyone could see that. Anyone could make a judgement about it.

But if a painting were some abstract, where does its truth lie? And who could make a judgement about it?

Kitty: You know, you are like Michael Collins. You're straight forward in a roundabout way. It cost him his life. [*Pause*] You didn't answer my question.

Lomax: Your question is a trap. There's truth in the state of real pregnancy and truth in the fake. What about this war? Is it truer to say that it should be fought or that it shouldn't? That is a trap too. Attempt to answer it and you might find yourself on the side opposite from the one you believe in. I am more interested in the effect of the war.

Kitty: You can't be. You've disowned it.

Lomax: No! I was never a part of it.

Kitty: That's like a mother denying she's part of the baby she bears.

Lomax: It's like denying she's a party to its death. [*Short pause*] What I most object to about this war is that its outcome could be seen before it began.

Kitty: You mean you know who's going to win?

Lomax: No. That makes no difference. What I mean is that it will be the end of European representationalism. In all its manifestations and with all its effects.

Kitty: Well I can tell you, when Collins - THROUGH NO FAULT OF HIS OWN - failed to settle the Irish troubles by signing his British treaty it was because the Carsonites in Ulster, the Irish Conservatives on the farms, the Redmonites, the blacklegs and every other whoreson rebel-against-the-cause wanted representation. So maybe it'll be no bad thing!

[*Silence*]

Lomax: Keep still. I can't get your nose.

Kitty: [*Laughing ironically*] He's trying to catch my nose like the gentry would catch butterflies! What about Percy? He's not catching any butterflies. Let me ask you one thing: supposing you knew Percy's life was in danger. Would you help him?

[*Silence*]

Lomax: You can't make your decision to come here; your decision to stay, a factor in my life because it suits you for it to be so.

Kitty: [*Becoming angry*] Not...well - forget about Percy - I just want to know. Tell me. You can tell me that. Would you help anybody? Any other conscientious objector?

[*Silence*]

Lomax: If I were to help your Mr Smith and lose my own life, that would be to promote the kind of senseless waste I am objecting to.

[*KITTY jumps up*]

Kitty: You're not objecting to anything! You'll use any argument to keep your own little individual self safe. It's all lies and fallacy! You're no Michael Collins. What good is it to be an individual in a world where all else is rotting bodies!

[*She storms off*]

[*LOMAX sighs. He shakes his head*]

[*He stands back to look at canvas. He makes a couple of amendments*]

[*He pauses*]

[*He listens carefully*]

[*He goes off*]

[*He returns a moment later with BRAUN*]

[*He is holding BRAUN by the ear*]

[*BRAUN is squealing*]

Lomax: Braun. Herr Braun. Representative Braun of the world's cuckoo. A fake cuckoo at that: cuckoo only in shape; only in appearance; the body, the reality is the school of the multitudinous termite. The WHITE ANT!

[*He pushes BRAUN away. He kicks him on the arse as he does so*]

Braun: [*Backing off. With accent*] I know what this means Lomax! I will get you! You will see! You will be got!

[*LOMAX laughs*]

[*BRAUN scuttles off*]

[*Lights down*]

Scene Seven

Scene: *DANGERFIELD is sitting in a deck chair next to his desk in field.*
He has his shirt sleeves rolled up and collar tucked in.
He has a large handkerchief over his head.
The trouser leg on his good leg is rolled up and the other one is down.

Braun: [*Off*] Colonial!

[*DANGERFIELD doesn't move*]

[*BRAUN comes on*]

Braun: [*With accent*] Ah, you English! If you can't bring the English to the seaside you must bring the seaside to the English!

[*OPERARTI comes on*]

[*OPERARTI wears only trunks or underpants*]

Braun: Operarti!...What...? You look like pimp!

Operarti: [*With accent. Superiorly*] You are uncultured.

Braun: Uncultured! [*To DANGERFIELD*] Actually Colonial, this is just why I come to see you. I am great writer of next, post war, generation. Great post-Freudian writer...

Operarti: And I am Italian! In Italy, the great living art of the people is making babies. It is the art of the fascio di combattimento. And I am great artist!

Braun: The point is Colonial, do you know that Lomax has the woman? I mean today he has had the woman with him, painting her.

[*Silence*]

Braun: He is neo-classicist!

Dangerfield: Who?

Braun: Lomax.

Dangerfield: You mean his landscapes?

Braun: I mean his [*Twists finger at his head*] philosophy.

Dangerfield: I thought his Beach at Blackpool was quite modern.

Braun: Ah yes, modern with classical ideas.

Dangerfield: Surely you Germans are the new Romans.

Braun: No. We are much more modern than that. I, for example, am Post Freudian. FREUDian.

Dangerfield: Are you suggesting, Braun, that Lomax the Englishman is a neo-classicist while the Germans are allies of the avant-garde?

Braun: [*Proudly*] We are allies of Nietzsche who is ally of Freud. That is our allies. The point is, Lomax will not help you win the war because he is neo-classicist and whoever wins we live in Post Freudian world. Then he will be out of work. So, who should be most favoured with woman in this world just before end of war which will bring Post Freudianism, the neo-Classicist or [*Beating his chest*] the Post Freudian!

Operarti: Or the great Italian baby maker!

Braun: It is almost so rational that nearly I can't believe it!

[*Silence*]

Dangerfield: What do you want me to do?

Braun: Deprive him.

Operarti: Take off his balls!

[*Silence*]

Dangerfield: I can't do it.

Braun: Why not?

Dangerfield : Because I would be condemned.

Operarti: Condemned?

Dangerfield: For a prejudice against conscientious objectors.

Braun: [*Incredulously*] You?

Operarti: It is not possible!

Dangerfield: No, no, Gentleman, it's out of the question.

Braun: [*Furious*] What can be done! [*Pause. He calms*] Forgive me Colonial. It is not because he is conscientious objector is it? It is because he is English.

Dangerfield: [*Sitting up*] That is entirely unfair Braun. No one is more conscientious in the condemning of the bad English than the English themselves.

Braun: But in this case the bad English is conscientious himself! One kind of conscientious English is condemning another kind of conscientious English! If there is a kind of conscientious English who should be condemned and he isn't then he must be unconscientious - that's Lomax. Is he UNconscientious objector? But if he is and you don't condemn him, it means YOU TOO Herr Colonial, are unconscientious. If you can find out what he is, if you can find out if he is unconscientious objector, then you must condemn him.

[*Silence*]

Dangerfield: A black act.

Braun: What?

Dangerfield: You must conceive a black act to challenge him. Though, I think you will find, as with the monstrous black act your countries have imposed on the world, the Englishman will win.

[*DANGERFIELD gets up*]

[*He looks off*]

Dangerfield: [*Pointing*] Operarti, are you having a mutiny?

Braun: Please Colonial! You must put it down or his Italians will effect the whole of our axis. We need to know whose soil is whose. You see! Look! [*Points*] Already there are more going down. Are they striking? Only this would be so typical of Mussolini's pink fascism!

Operarti: [*Angrily*] Perhaps they are dying! They are thirsty!

Dangerfield: [*Also angry*] They're not dying! [*Shouting to off*] You men! Get up! I want this field prepared before the rain comes!

[*He goes off*]

[*BRAUN paces a little preoccupied*]

[*OPERARTI looks off also preoccupied*]

Braun: [*Without accent*] Operarti, do you believe Lomax is screwing the girl?

Operarti: [*With accent*] He said he was. I told her he said he was.

Braun: Which means you must have believed he was. You're not the kind of person to tell a lie.

Operarti: No.

Braun: But you said that you didn't think he would do it because she's pregnant.

Operarti: I know. I believed the English to be more honourable.

Braun: Well in a sense, you see, you're right. Now listen... [*Pause*] Promise me...promise me on the life of Mrs Mussolini...

Operarti: [*Dismayed*] Mrs Mussolini! But what is wrong with Mrs Operarti?

Braun: I didn't know you were married.

Operarti: My mother! Mama mia!

Braun: Promise me, on your mother's life, that you won't tell anyone what I am about to tell you.

Operarti: I promise.

[*Pause*]

Braun: She's not pregnant!

[*OPERARTI looks shocked*]

Braun: It's straw. It's fake. A pretence!

Operarti: [*Sadly*] No baby?

Braun: No baby. But this is the beauty. This is what we'll do...

Operarti: Lieutenant Braun, I don't know what to believe any more.

Braun: Did you ever know what to believe?

[*OPERARTI looks blank*]

Braun: Just listen. I've got a little plan - a way we can get that big bastard Lomax once and for all. The girl will be helping us. Dangerfield is on our side. A black act has come to me: a coal black, BOOT black, black act. It'll work. [*Pause*] The only way we can really get Lomax is to disembowel him - metaphorically speaking - in front of Dangerfield. We'll have the baby - She'll have the baby and she'll give the baby to me. Right? Everybody will believe that the baby is real. Right? Then YOU, just before the act, must tell Lomax that the baby is fake: a doll. Do you understand?

Operarti: No.

Braun: But you know what to do?

Operarti: Yes.

Braun: You just don't know why you've got to do it.

Operarti: No.

Braun: And this is a twentieth century reality?

Operarti: Yes.

Braun: It's more than that Vittorio! It's Post Freudian! You don't NEED to know. Whatever happens to you in this life is just an accumulation of the accidental concurrences of influences from a variety of sources. You can class yourself with your king - Victor Emmanuel. We, the Germans and Italians are lucky: we have leaders who are prepared to shoulder the responsibility of this badminton shuttle-cock theory of history. You can sum it up in a sentence: whatever happens to Lomax he's got coming. Please Vittorio, don't let us down. You have to find a time to tell him when you know that the opportunity for him to tell Dangerfield is passed. Do you see? Put simply: when the black act comes, we want Dangerfield to believe the doll is a baby and Lomax to believe the baby is a doll.

Operarti: The BABY is a doll?

Braun: I'm sorry. Quite correct. You're right to correct me - we want Lomax to believe, to KNOW, that the doll is a doll. OK?

Operarti: [*Sighing*] OK.

Braun: [*Perplexed*] Vittorio.

Operarti: No, it OK. I can do it. I know how important. It just...you know. I am Mama boy. For me, I lay on her lap and suck tit and it could heaven be. And Papa, he does garden and sun is hot. You see? [*Indicates off*] It how I can do this. But now this Kitty, she make my life different. [*Pause*] You want to get Lomax? Not hurt Kitty because she shagged with Lomax?

Braun: Good heavens! What are you suggesting!

Operarti: [*Tentatively*] The baby...

Braun: [*Authoritarianly*] The DOLL!

Operarti: It is OK. I believe.

Braun: [*Indicating off*] Look Vittorio. Your Italians have seen you. They are returning. They respect you. Respect yourself. See how well they've planted and landscaped the field? What we have to do to Lomax is part of the same landscaping plan.

[*Silence*]

[*They look off*]

[*BRAUN shakes his head*]

Braun: Dangerfield. [*Dismissive noise*] These English! You know the difference, Vittorio, between Hitler and someone like Dangerfield? [*Pause*] Dangerfield, the Englishman, will take a weekend in the country, Hitler will take a country in a weekend.

[*Silence*]

[*Lights down*]

Scene Eight

Scene: *The Barn. Night.*

KITTY is asleep.

[*BRAUN creeps on*]

[*He comes to KITTY. He kneels beside her and listens to her breathing*]

[*He takes his clothes off*]

[*He gets into KITTY's 'bed'*]

Kitty: [*In her sleep*] Percy...it's too late...

[*BRAUN rolls her gently onto her back*]

Kitty: [*Groggily*] Perc...Percy!

[*BRAUN gets over her. He kisses KITTY*]

[KITTY wakes]

Kitty; *[Shocked]* What are you...!

[She struggles]

[BRAUN gets off her quickly like a schoolboy caught - as if he wasn't doing it]

[Silence]

[KITTY suddenly sits up]

Kitty: What are you doing here?!

Braun: *[With accent]* I want the baby.

[KITTY beats BRAUN on the chest]

Kitty: *[Angrily. Tearfully]* You've got no feelings! You'd use anything to get your way - even a baby that can't be born!

[BRAUN gets away from her]

Braun: *[With accent]* It is not true! Don't believe it! It is said violent nationalism is because of sexual impotence. I don't believe that. You are beautiful. That is what I believe.

[Silence]

[KITTY subsides]

Braun: *[Ingratiatingly]* It is said nationalism is substitute for sex. It is not true. Nationalism is sublimation of sex. This is why I do not want to give you a baby but instead you give it to me.

[KITTY lays down]

Braun: I must have baby...of course, not a real baby - I have doll but - you know...*[Pause]* You must not love Lomax.

[KITTY looks at BRAUN angrily]

Braun: Lomax belongs to same people who hanged Roger Casement. When I see you arguing with him I know you are in love...

Kitty: You know nothing of the sort!

Braun: *[Sulkingly]* I know this arguing with him is sign of love.

Kitty: You do not. We - you and I - are arguing but that is NOT a sign of love. You can have the baby! *[Pause]* Then I can see Percy and clear off out of here.

[Silence]

Braun: *[With accent]* What will happen - we must get Lomax to come here to barn, tomorrow night at twelve of clock. Midnight. And you will see; we will all see...ssssh!

[*Silence*]

[*He collects his clothes*]

Braun: Do you hear? Do you hear that walk? I must hide!

[*He rushes off with his clothes*]

[*DANGERFIELD comes on*]

[*DANGERFIELD wears a collar and tie as though he's come courting*]

Dangerfield: [*As he comes on*] Kitty?

Kitty: Yes?

[*DANGERFIELD offers KITTY a small parcel*]

Dangerfield: Sandlewood soap. From India. [*Pause*] For you.

[*Silence*]

[*DANGERFIELD breathes deep. He stands awkwardly*]

Dangerfield: You know...[*Pause*] The English in India. The way some people talk...they speak of rape. A ravishment. A ravishment of this great hot country by lesser beings from a colder clime. They argue that history in the future - will be the victories of lesser people. And so the history of the future will be the rape of great peoples by lesser ones. [*Suddenly angry*] Well who are they talking about? Who's the lesser person here? Do they know what ravishment is? Are they talking about fucking?

[*KITTY groans*]

Dangerfield: I'm sorry I forgot myself...[*A little angry again*] But I ask myself this: have the English merely fucked India? We've built great buildings there! We've celebrated Maharajas! We eat curry; we drink tea. If this is fucking why shouldn't people generally do it? If fucking mixes cultures then ravishment is far-sightedness! Kitty! I need you!

[*KITTY's groans grow*]

Dangerfield: Kitty! I'm a man!

Kitty: You're English! Save yourself! You wouldn't want this!

[*She cries out*]

Dangerfield: What is it?

Kitty: My baby...Oh! Leave us! Don't help me! Go!

Dangerfield: Shouldn't I...?

Kitty: [*Cries out*] No! The baby is Irish! Half-breed! ...Irish and conscientious objector!

[*DANGERFIELD is horror struck*]

Kitty: You would only hate yourself if you helped and that wouldn't help all those you already hate. There is only one thing...[*She gasps, cries out, pants...*] Percy. I must see Percy. Don't worry. You'll have Lomax. You can see him here tomorrow night at midnight.

[*DANGERFIELD comes to KITTY who has her legs drawn up before her - The posture of a woman in labour*]

[*He pauses*]

[*He turns away suddenly, biting his fists with frustration*]

[*Pause*]

Dangerfield: You can see Smith tomorrow night at the same time. Then I want you to take that baby and go.

[*KITTY's false labour pains continue*]

Dangerfield: Ask for the long field. Go to the top of the field by midnight and you will see two men. They will take you to see Smith...

Kitty: It's coming!

[*She lets out a terrible cry*]

[*DANGERFIELD cries out in horror and rushes off*]

[*After a short time BRAUN comes back on clothed*]

Braun: Quick, hurry!

[*BRAUN rips the straw out of KITTY's belly*]

Braun: What if he sends camp doctor! No, no! We don't want. We take straw out and we wrap you like...[*Hesitation*] baby in blanket. Like colossal napkin.

[*Pause*]

[*KITTY touches BRAUN's face*]

Kitty: When the war's over, Helmut, get married and have some babies.

Braun: [*Without accent. Looking into her eyes*] I hate this. This is sad - ripping her baby out. But what's sadder. She's come to see Smith. What will she see? [*Pause. Suddenly angry with himself*] Look at it another way...!

Kitty: You shouldn't speak German. It makes you angry. It's an angry tongue. We won't do the napkin. It's a bit silly.

Braun: [*Without accent*] If she hadn't come to see Smith and yet she was here, why would she be here?

[*KITTY sighs*]

Braun: What would this woman be doing in a world of men? A world at war is a world of men rampant. That's all there is to it. Women are kept out so that we can concentrate on the fight. Any losses will be notified by letter.

Kitty: I'll stay out of sight for the day. If a doctor came he'd wonder where me baby was. You've got YOUR baby. I'll see Percy tomorrow night and then I'll be gone.

Braun: [*With accent*] You are right. We will do it this way. I can tell Lomax that you want to see him here because you have had a baby and he is the only person you trust...OK?

[*BRAUN gets up*]

[*KITTY suddenly looks worried*]

Kitty: Wait.

[*BRAUN pauses*]

Kitty: Not "trust".

Braun Not trust? OK.

[*KITTY turns away*]

[*BRAUN goes off*]

[*Lights down*]

Scene Nine

Scene: *The Barn. Midnight.*

DANGERFIELD is hidden watching BRAUN.

BRAUN is wearing a sheet like a druid's shroud.

BRAUN has put the coffin on two supporting objects.

He piles hay beneath the coffin.

DANGERFIELD comes on.

Dangerfield: What are you doing?

Braun: [*Happily*] Hello Colonial. O, this will be sacrifice. Immolation. You know? And also, I will show you what Lomax is.

[*Silence*]

Braun: You don't understand? It is simple! You want rain - I will make some. I believe in this rain: it brings a kind of living space.

You know? Without rain the field is dead - a kind of dying space. With rain, it is alive; it grows. I will make a kind of Pagan rite. You know? As in Richard Strauss or Richard Wagner. This music is ritual. Yes? We go back to go forward.

Dangerfield: Explain the ritual.

Braun: O, it is nothing. Just small. Well first I say something - you know...abracadabra..bbbvvvt...then I make the sacrifice with knife and then I burn the hay with the sacrifice.

Dangerfield: Which is what?

Braun: [*Bemused*] What is which what?

Dangerfield: What are you sacrificing?

Braun: O, Kitty's baby.

Dangerfield: You've got Kitty's baby?

Braun: Yes.

Dangerfield: Where is it?

Braun: Asleep.

Dangerfield: You stole it?

Braun: You hate it. It betrayed you.

Dangerfield: What do you mean?

Braun: You wanted...[*Makes pumping action with his arm*] And the baby came and stopped you. You see? The thought of the baby makes you sick. The thought of what a woman's body is really for makes you sick. So you hate the baby. The baby brought you back from your world of raping fantasies to real world.

Dangerfield: How would you know these things?

Braun: She told me. When she gave me baby.

Dangerfield: She gave you the baby?

Braun: Yes.

Dangerfield: To kill?

Braun: Yes.

Dangerfield: Impossible!

Braun: Why? [*Pause*] Look: I said, the baby will give you grief. You think of Percy Smith. He is here because he is conscientious objector. His wife or his woman is having a baby. Would he be conscientious if he left his wife and baby alone in middle of war? He doesn't have to fight. He can do non-combatant work. I said:

no, this baby is no good for Percy Smith. If he is not conscientious how can he be a conscientious objector? I said: this is war; we have to give up many things, including family life and babies. Bombs drop you know...babies die all over. We can begin again when war is dead and babies can live. And you will find, I said, that if you sacrifice - well I didn't use that word - too harsh - then I said, Percy Smith will have unexpected benefit. But, of course, we will corner Lomax like a rat! I will sacrifice baby and, he will do nothing to stop it. Sssshhhh! I hear...I have good ear...! It must be him; it is heavy step. You go back into dark.

[*DANGERFIELD backs into dark*]

[*LOMAX comes slowly on not comprehending what he sees*]

[*He pauses*]

Braun: [*Like a priest*] Wie durch Fluch er mir geriet, verflucht sei dieser Ring!

[*Silence*]

[*BRAUN goes from coffin and picks up a small bundle*]

[*He takes bundle to coffin and places it in*]

[*He draws a knife which he holds high*]

Lomax: Wait a minute Braun. What have you put in that coffin?

Braun: [*Pausing with mock shock*] SsssHHH! It's Kitty's doll.

Lomax: Doll! That's Kitty's baby!

Operarti: [*Off, with accent*] I am love to Kitty! I am love her baby!

[*LOMAX goes for BRAUN as BRAUN plunges knife into coffin*]

[*At same moment as LOMAX moves for BRAUN, ie just before the knife enters the coffin, OPERARTI rushes on shouting*]

Operarti: [*With accent*] I don't believe you Braun! The baby is real!

[*OPERARTI stops suddenly*]

Operarti: It is done?

Braun: [*Scornfully. Without accent*] Yes, it's done Operarti. The doll is dead.

Operarti: [*Shakes LOMAX. With accent*] I hate you Mussolini! You bastard! You stole my thoughts! I couldn't think to save baby!

[*KITTY screams off*]

[*OPERARTI pulls at his hair*]

Operarti: [*With accent*] No more I don't believe in NOT believing! No more I don't know what belief! I denounce d'Anunnzio! The doll is dead!

[*OPERARTI rushes off*]

[*BRAUN takes doll from coffin. He holds it up by the knife*]

Braun: Look! Ha! It is doll!

[*BRAUN drops doll in coffin*]

[*DANGERFIELD comes out of the dark*]

[*DANGERFIELD shoots LOMAX*]

[*LOMAX falls*]

[*BRAUN looks surprised*]

Braun: But he tried to save baby! Isn't this English?

Dangerfield: An Irish baby! Get some men and arrest him.

Braun: But he is dead.

Dangerfield: I winged him.

[*BRAUN kneels by LOMAX*]

[*LOMAX groans*]

Dangerfield: An Irish baby! Arrest the fucker. While English babies are being slaughtered in their beds...Wait, Braun...

Braun: [*Standing*] I will gladly arrest him. I would be better to take him out in coffin, but.....

Dangerfield: Braun...!

Braun: No, wait. I must tell you this: Adolf Hitler has a beautiful mind. He says this: he says the new age is so new it is like ameoba. It is simple, basic single cell made up of mass of men. Like a cell in his own brain! Hitler has a beautiful brain. He says: the millenium is here. It is an ameoba millenium. The mass that makes cell is all there is. If there is individual outside, Hitler says the mass will arrest him and like in the ameoba, the mass arrests the individual - engulfs him and the individual becomes the mass.

Dangerfield: Braun! Shut this bollocks up! This sacrifice...there's not going to be any rain is there? I mean the baby was rubber...

Braun: [*Surprised*] No! No rain!

Dangerfield: Shit.

Braun: But no rain if baby was...

Dangerfield: Bugger! Bugger! Bugger! [*Paces*] I had hoped... just for a

few minutes then, a short time, I had hoped...I thought we had it!
RAIN! Nazi fart! Not only an Irish baby, NOT a baby!

[*KITTY rushes on*]

[*Beside herself, she strikes DANGERFIELD*]

Kitty: It wasn't an Irish baby! It was a British baby! It was the baby of six British soldiers!

Braun: But it was a doll!

[*DANGERFIELD pulls gun*]

Dangerfield: Hold this bitch off!

Braun: You hold her!

Dangerfield: What?

Braun: You insult me you limey snot!

[*KITTY sinks to ground and kneels beside LOMAX*]

Braun: You think I could kill REAL baby! What you think I am?

[*KITTY is sobbing*]

Dangerfield: You're a kraut!

Braun: I am noble German warrior...!

Dangerfield: You're a kraut!

Kitty: Percy's dead. I've just seen him. His body. In the field. Two Italians were there. They showed me the hole in the field. They said the field is full of bodies. [*To LOMAX directly*] Did you know?

Lomax: [*Coming to*] Am I bleeding?

Dangerfield: [*Putting his gun away*] There's no blood. There never is is there Lomax? Cleaner than a line of logic.

Kitty: Did you know Percy was dead?

Braun: Lomax knew. He is English mad bastard like this one. He say: execution is occupational hazard of conscientious objector!

Dangerfield: Braun! Shut this bollocks up! I don't want to hear it! My head's spinning.

Braun: You won't hear it! It OK. I tell you why. I'm fucked off. I will arrest....

Dangerfield: Shut up!

[*DANGERFIELD takes out a letter*]

[*He lets it drop on KITTY*]

Dangerfield: Here's Smith's last letter...the last relic of a lost...a lost what? [*Pause*] A lost what! Ha! Ha!

Kitty: [*Fearfully*] A letter! I can't...

[*She holds letter tightly*]

Lomax: [*Weakly*] Have you got something to put under my head?

Dangerfield: We'll call the field: the field of the lost whats! Ha! Ha! The field of the lost whats! The long field of the lost....The field of the LONG LOST whats! Ha, Ha...!

Kitty: [*Tearfully*] I came here to tell Percy I hate him! That's why I came. I was going to see him face to face; tell him I hate him and spit in his face!

Braun: [*Embarrassed*] You want I should arrest woman also?

Dangerfield: Arrest! I want that you should subsume Braun! Become again part of that mass of war's offal that being German has bred you for.

[*DANGERFIELD goes towards coffin*]

[*BRAUN looks numb*]

Kitty: I can't read it. It would be too close...it would be like a haemorrhage. No. I haven't got anything to put under your head. [*Pause*] Do you want to read my letter?

[*There is no reaction from LOMAX*]

Dangerfield: Arrest! Christ, we haven't lost the war have we?

[*DANGERFIELD hits BRAUN on the head*]

[*BRAUN exaggerates his fall*]

Kitty: No, you don't! Because it's got blood on it. I suppose you've never seen the blood of war! The dead men in the field.

Dangerfield: [*About BRAUN. Scoffingly*] 20th Century German! Felled like an oak from a tap on his acorn!

Kitty: That's why you paint portraits of healthy women! You're not interested in the real world. Life for you on this camp has only been a representation. That's how you can paint the portrait of a pregnant woman who's not pregnant!

Dangerfield: [*At coffin*] Baba, baba...

[*He puts his hands into coffin as if he were about to pick out a real baby*]

Kitty: There WAS a baby. [*Short pause*] While I was pregnant, Percy's mother saved me. Me and Percy fell in love but he left me when he found out about the child.

[*DANGERFIELD holds doll gently as if it were a real baby*]

Dangerfield: Baba, baba...

Kitty: Then it died. Then I stayed with Mrs Smith. And she was hated because Percy wouldn't fight.

[*DANGERFIELD begins struggling with the knife in the doll - trying to take it out*]

Kitty: I often wondered whether he left because the baby was the baby of six British soldiers, but it wasn't true. Not six. Just one ravaged boy. Maybe he left me because I was a coward.

[*KITTY gets up quickly*]

[*She begins to go off, confused and unhappy etc.*]

[*DANGERFIELD pulls knife out of doll and looks at it madly*]

Lomax: [*Weakly*] Where are you going?

Kitty: My shawl. I forgot...I left it with Percy.

Lomax: Leave it! It's too dark!

Kitty: [*Angrily*] Don't you want your head wrapped!

[*She goes off*]

Dangerfield: [*To BRAUN who is cowering resentfully*] Look how you knifed the fucker! I've got a good mind...

[*DANGERFIELD holds knife at BRAUN's throat*]

[*He throws knife away*]

[*OPERARTI lets out a cry off*]

Operarti: [*Off. Tragically*] Eia, eia, alala!

[*There is a dull thud as he drops*]

[*DANGERFIELD cradles doll happily humming*]

Braun: [*Shocked*] Operarti! Vittorio!

[*DANGERFIELD rocks doll and sings*]

Dangerfield: Send him victorious, happy and glorious, long to reign over us...ha! Ha!

[*He goes off singing and rocking doll as he does*]

Dangerfield: [*Going off*] Send clouds victorious, happy and glorious, long to rain over us, God save the King....

Braun: [*Shouting after DANGERFIELD almost tearfully*] I am now seen it Dangerfield! You are mad, so mad I have faith no more in irrational! It is finished! Finished!

[*BRAUN goes off*]

[*After a moment, LOMAX gets up with difficulty*]

[*He goes to coffin and looks at it*]

[*He suddenly, angrily, kicks it over*]

[*He sits beside the fallen coffin*]

[*KITTY comes on*]

[*She has dirt on her face. She looks empty*]

Kitty: Vittorio. What does it mean? Victory?

[*She goes to LOMAX*]

Kitty: Victory means that someone's been killed.

[*She begins to bandage LOMAX with shawl*]

Kitty: You know...[*She pauses*] Hitler and Mussolini and Churchill and Stalin, they're a sideshow. [*Pause*] I've just kissed death. I climbed into the grave. I got into the grave and I kissed him. I kissed him. I kissed him and his face caved in. I've got Percy's flesh on me lips! Is that war or is it something more terrible?

Lomax: It's war. As bad as that. Worse than it's been painted.

[*Lights go out. Moonlight*]

[*KITTY stops bandaging*]

[*She gets up and begins to move in circles feeling her way as if she were in a glass box: almost as if she were blind*]

Kitty: [*With fear in her voice*] So, Percy was right. Hitler and Mussolini, Churchill and Stalin, they're just the side show; as if he knew one day he'd give up the flesh from his bone. Follow me.

[*BRAUN comes on carrying the dead OPERARTI*]

[*He moves very slowly*]

[*OPERARTI has a rope around his neck*]

[*LOMAX remains where he is*]

Kitty: I'm finding my way out. Christ it's frightening. It's frightening how funny it is. I'm looking into that hole, that grave, falling in of my own accord. I'm seeing the hole in Ireland where they lowered Collins. It's a hole as big as the Irish Sea. And Collins' face is coming up out of the sea like the whole of bloody Ireland! And he's laughing at me! Follow me!

[*She keeps feeling the air*]

Kitty: They're just the sideshow. This big face is coming up out of the ocean and it's laughing. The sea is full of rain! FOLLOW! Christ, I've got to get out of here. And you should come. That would be a good thing to decide to do. Jesus, I'm frightened of me own vision! [*Short pause*] You know what's happened to me? Percy has spoken from the grave and told me the truth. And now for the first time I can feel certain about Collins and say that when he died he'd gone into the war to fight the fighting of it. That's why all sides joined in his wake.

[*She turns very quickly to LOMAX*]

Kitty: Come on, you've got to follow! We've got to get out of here fence or no fence. This big fucking laughing face is coming up. Not mocking! The laughing face of a ghost. The ghost of a big fellow who was wasted. He's laughing at the main attraction. At this mad, mad Englishman who's planted other Englishmen! Planted them like plants to have the English rain fall on them. To have them fertilized with Englishness. So that they will sing and fuck and fight and die in unison! [*She laughs*] Am I right?

Lomax: [*Getting up*] Yes.

[*KITTY has reached the moonlight*]

Kitty: Can you paint it?

[*She begins to go*]

Lomax: Kitty!

[*She pauses*]

[*LOMAX goes to her*]

Lomax: Let me read the letter.

[*They go off*]

[*BRAUN remains rocking the dead OPERARTI*]

[*Lights down*]

END